THE FRENCH METHOD

Lose weight and live longer

Emeric Lebreton
Doctor in psychology

THANKS

---

*First I would like to express my deepest gratitude to all
my patients who have helped me with their amazing
stories and their exemplary path to success, which has
helped me define an effective way of losing weight
in the long term. I would also like to thank Valériane,
the dietician and nutritionist at our centre, with whom
I developed this program. Without her help, none of this
would have been possible. She's an amazing person.
I would also like to thank Béatrice for the time spent
editing this book to ensure its language is impeccable.
Without her it would never have been published as
quickly as it was. Finally, I must pay homage to Jim
Morrison, whose inspiring songs and music have been
my faithful companions while writing this book.
He gave me my sense of irreverence and anti-conformity.*

Let food be thy medicine!

Hippocrates

CONTENTS

STAGE 3: UNDERSTANDING YOUR EXCESS WEIGHT AND WHAT YOU NEED TO DO TO LOSE IT

STAGE 1:

MAKING A LONG-TERM COMMITMENT

ARE YOU REALLY SURE YOU WANT TO READ THIS BOOK?

So, you've bought this book. Before you start reading I'd like to ask you one thing: are you really sure you want to read it?

I'm asking this for a very good reason: this book will change your life for good.

Maybe you told yourself, I bought this book to lose 10 kg (22 pounds), not to change my life. In this case, I recommend you take it back to the book shop and get your money back.

Because this isn't a diet book. It's not intended to give you the strength to deprive yourself for months, eating correctly only to return to your bad habits and gain your hard-lost pounds back in a few weeks. You know as well as I that when it comes to diets, you always gain more than you lose!

So, some patients have told me that they've spent their life on a diet. Since the age of 15, every 5 years they have lost 22 pounds only to gain 15 kg (33 pounds) back each time, with predictable results. They came to me desperate to find a solution, exhausted by all these useless diets.

Going on a diet normally involves a temporary lifestyle change before returning to normal as if nothing has happened. Unfortunately, the same causes have the same effects.

The trouble with overweight people is not the food they eat, it's their lifestyle. It's their habits, their beliefs, their lifestyle and above all their relationship with food. The trouble is, this lifestyle is considered normal by way too many people.

That's why 40% of people in the world are overweight and almost 15% of people are obese!

This book aims to help you change your lifestyle for good. That's why I prefer to be sure you're not labouring under any misapprehensions before we start on this path.

If you really want to change your life for good, lose weight, eat more healthily and live better and longer, then this book is for you. If you just want to go on a diet and keep the same old habits, there's still time to realise your mistake and choose another book and another therapist.

Because reading this book means committing to lasting change. It's up to you whether you accept this change.

Otherwise, return this book to your bookshop and ask to swap it or get your money back.
If you accept the challenge, it means you're ready, able to question yourself and make a profound change.

You're one of those people who consider food to be the best path to happiness and a long life. In this case, we can start working together.

Think carefully, because once you've reached your decision, you can't go back. If you turn the page, it means you're ready.

This means you're ready to change, and change the world we live in.

THE COMMITMENTS YOU MAKE BY CHOOSING TO READ THIS BOOK

You've chosen to read this book. This means you are capable of change, questioning yourself, changing your habits and the way you think.

I'm delighted because I like to think I'm like that too. As I see it, the ability to change is the first quality an individual should develop, and something we should teach our children.
We are living beings, and isn't the main characteristic of life its incredible capacity to adapt?
But know this – by choosing to read this book, you're not only committing to spend time reading it carefully. You also need to make a commitment to follow the advice it gives, to do what is asked of you and face the challenges it contains.

This book is full of challenges that are not always easy to rise to, which require time, courage and energy.

1. Are you ready to do what's needed? Can you really commit to a permanent lifestyle change?
2. Answer these ten questions to find out:
3. Are you ready to listen to expert advice?
4. Are you ready to change your habits?

5. Are you ready to change the way you think?
6. Are you ready to make a lasting change?
7. Are you ready to accept the consequences of your weight loss?
8. Are you prepared for how people will look at you when you change?
9. Are you ready to learn to say NO?
10. Are you ready to transform yourself?
11. Are you ready to resist the pressure of the agro-food industry?
12. Are you ready to become a different person?

If you answered "YES" to all these questions, you're ready to start this book. Reading it will make you 100% sure of reaching your goal.

If you answered "NO" to any of these questions, take some time to reflect before reading this book.

Again, nobody is forcing you to read it. You're free to do what you want and choose another method to lose weight.

If you're really sure you want to read this book, evolve, change and transform yourself for good, and that "YES" is profound and sincere, then what are you waiting for?

Let's start work. I'm delighted to work with you. I already know we share a certain number of values, objectives and ideals.

Nobody will be prouder than me when you've lost the weight you wanted.

ABOUT ME:
WHY I WROTE THIS BOOK

My name is Emeric Lebreton. I'm a doctor in psychology.

Diet is normally a matter reserved for nutritionists. However, experience has taught me that we all know, more or less, what we need to do to eat a healthy, and balanced diet. We've all read a ton of articles written by experts explaining how we should eat, how much and at what time of the day.

We all know we're supposed to eat fruits and vegetables and limit sugary drinks and fatty, sugary or salty foods. We all know what to do, but often it's easier said than done.
Why are we unable to follow these recommendations?

To put it bluntly, because our brains fall short – diet is really a matter of psychology rather than medicine or nutrition.

Because someone who has food cravings and eats a whole cake every evening after watching an advert on TV knows they shouldn't do it. They know what's in that cake. They know there's too much sugar and fat in it. They know, but they can't stop themselves.

And faced with this, what can a nutritionist or dietician do?

Not much, other than to say: "You shouldn't have done that! Next time you're really hungry, eat carrots or radishes instead!"

Here I must apologise for my unfair caricature of the great work carried out by nutritionists.
Nevertheless, I will allow myself to give a few notable examples to demonstrate a reality which in France, a country dominated by traditional medicine, many people have trouble understanding:

**90% OF WEIGHT PROBLEMS ARE DUE
TO PSYCHOLOGY AND NOT DIET.**

This is why my skills here are so important in breaking the impasse. Because psychology as a science and as a technique enables action.

It allows us, using techniques that have proven their worth over more than a century, to change our behaviour, habits and ways mind-sets that are the cause of serious health problems, for good.
Psychology lets us:

- Transform a food addiction in the form of frequent cravings into indifference, indeed disgust,
- Get someone who's never done sport in their life onto an exercise bike,
- Transform a diet based on sugars and fats into a balanced diet full of fruits and vegetables,
- Reduce the anxiety and stress that so often make us seek solace in food,

- Help us better manage our emotions, which are key to regulating our appetite.

I've tested these techniques on hundreds of patients in my practice. And each time they were a success.

By choosing to read this book, you've chosen to benefit from these techniques.
The aim of this book is none other than making these techniques available to as many people as possible.

Every day I am struck by the despair, suffering and illnesses caused by malnutrition, and one of its most common manifestations, over-nutrition.

After suffering from famine for centuries, much of the human race has now fallen victim to a chronic excess of food. And this excess causes terrible illnesses like diabetes, hypertension, strokes, heart attacks and morbid obesity.

These illnesses cause millions of deaths each year – many more than wars, plane crashes or major epidemics put together. More people die each year from too much food than die of hunger.
And when it comes to being overweight, I know of what I speak.

Between the age of 29 and 34, I put on almost 30 kg (66 pounds). I had picked up some bad habits, I was working too much, I'd stopped paying attention and I was giving in to terrible food cravings. I'd become fat and heavy.

I was out of breath when I climbed the stairs, I had terrible digestive problems and found it hard to go jogging, one of my favourite sports, because it was hard on my knees. At just thirty four years of age I was feeling half the man I had been.

I could see myself getting old at a rate of knots. I felt very, very poorly. I had pains everywhere. I was tired and depressed.

At the time, I didn't realise I was suffering because I was overweight. When you're overweight, it's not just your body but your soul which suffers. Food is a boon, but it can easily become a curse.
Later in this book we'll see how food has a huge impact on our mood, our attention span and our levels of anxiety or aggression. We are what we eat, and what we eat can make us happy or destroy us.

I lost those 30 kg and radically transformed my diet. Today my life has changed. So it's also my personal experience I want to share in this book.

I hope you'll find it helpful.

THINGS TO REMEMBER BEFORE YOU START

- Your partner would like you to look like a pin-up or a Chippendale. They keep making comments or criticising your weight. They'd like you to stop eating to look better.
- Your doctor has warned you about the health issues caused by being overweight. He's put you on a diet, waving the red flag after your last check-up.
- You took a test in a magazine which showed that your BMI (Body Mass Index) was over 25, putting you in the overweight category and indicating you need to take action to lose weight.

In life, there is never any shortage of people who want us to be a certain way. Society puts pressure on us at all levels to "fit the mould".

I'd like you to do something before you start this program.

I'd like you to tell all these people to get lost!

Tell them that what you do and how you want to be is up to you.

Nobody has the right to tell you what you should do.

They can give you advice, give you suggestions, but nobody can force you to do anything.

Only you can decide.

If you want to be overweight and curvy, if you want to drink fizzy drinks, eat crisps, bars of chocolate or chocolate spread all hours of the day and night, at the risk of destroying your health, then that's up to you.

You should do what you want. You're completely free to be and become what you want. This is your most fundamental right.

And of course this is why you bought this book. You bought this book because you're free and you decided to lose weight.

You made this choice for you and for you alone.

You didn't do it for your partner, your doctor or your friends, or to look like a cover star. It's all about you.

You're doing it because you feel like it.

You want to feel better in mind and body.

You fancy a taste of being thin.

You want to rediscover the pleasure of being in control of your body and doing what you want.

You'd like to wear the clothes you want. You want do dress how you want. Quite simply, you like to be free, and you feel being overweight restricts your freedom.

You're doing it because you like a challenge, and losing weight is your challenge.

You decided to follow this program because you want to be proud of achieving a goal: your goal.

And you already know you'll achieve it because you plan to equip yourself with the means to do so. You plan to take action, action leading to concrete results. You're capable of achieving great things.

You're capable of confronting all the challenges your day to day life brings. You're capable of losing this excess weight, which is no use to you and which is holding you back. Because you're making progress.

And buying this book is one way of expressing your decision and saying:

YES, I'M READY!

I'm in the mood. I have the will. I'm motivated and ready to take action here and now to achieve this goal.

Let's do it!

STAGE 2:
PREPARING FOR YOUR WEIGHT LOSS

PREPARING TO LOSE WEIGHT

When a top-level athlete wants to win an important competition, he trains for many months. When you plant a tree, you start by preparing the soil so the seed has all it needs to grow. When you climb a mountain, you take everything you need to survive with you. The rule is the same whatever the goal pursued. If you want to achieve a goal, you need to prepare yourself and ensure the conditions are there for success.

What happens if you fail to make adequate preparations?

Athletes risk injuring themselves during the competition and losing any chance of realising their dream. Seeds will be slow to grow, and the tree sickly and unable to bear fruit. As for mountain climbers, if they get caught by a storm and are unable to react, they'll be forced to give up half way, or worse, perish on the mountainside. Preparation is key. I'm sure you're in a hurry to obtain results and begin. But first you need to prepare yourself.

Preparation for the Psy'Action® method is based on 3 key actions that you can learn right away:

- **First of all, get your friends and family on side:** they can be your best friends or the worst enemies of change. If you don't prepare the ground, if you don't get them on side, they risk making you fail.

- **Next you need to prepare yourself mentally:** there are some practical exercises for this which will help you boost your motivation and perseverance, two essential qualities for success.
- **Finally, you need to do some housekeeping:** in concrete terms this means cleaning out your cupboards, getting rid of everything not worth eating, but also clearing your mind of any wrong beliefs.

So, let's find out how to prepare for weight loss and rebalance your relationship with food for good.

Don't forget! Losing weight for good means, to some extent, changing your life!

ACTION N°1:
GET YOUR FRIENDS AND FAMILY ON SIDE

Virginie has decided to lose weight!

Virginie is a young 19-year-old woman. She's one of those "curvy" young women. According to her GP, she's 20 kg overweight. Virginie is not comfortable in her own skin. She feels fat and unattractive. She wants to be popular with the boys like her best friend Pauline. Pauline has a model's figure. She's very popular with the boys. Virginie would like a boyfriend.

One day, Virginie decides to go on a diet. That's that, it's all decided, she's going to lose weight and do sport to sculpt her figure. Because she's worried she won't manage it, Virginie prefers not to tell anyone. So she starts her diet alone. On the second day her mum, a constant worrier, asks her if everything is ok. She seems to have lost her appetite. Has she got any problems? Virginie answers that everything is fine, and that she's just decided to lose a bit of weight. Her mother doesn't believe her. If she's not eating, it's obviously because something's wrong. She decides to see a psychiatrist. And over the next few days she cooks up a load of lovely little dishes to cheer her up.

Virginie goes to the psychiatrist who can't find anything wrong with her, and she somehow manages to refuse the dishes her mum absolutely insists she eats. She manages to lose 5 kg (11 lbs.). Now her friends start asking her if everything's ok. Everyone around her is worried at the change in her bubbly personality, offering her sweets to cheer her up. Everyone knows Virginie loves sweets. Of course Virginie is very tempted. But in the end she digs her heels in and finds the strength to say no. Rumours start to circulate: Virginie has a serious problem that she's hiding from everyone, clearly a serious illness!

Virginie is doing more and more sport. She loses 10 kg (22 lbs.) and above all her body is transformed – thinner, better defined, more contoured. Physically she's a different person. Finally she can wear fashionable and sexy clothes like Pauline.

Suddenly boys start to look at her differently, something which doesn't go unnoticed by Pauline. Because in their small circle of friends, Pauline is suddenly not always the centre of attention. The person who was her best friend, who would listen to her pour her heart out with eyes full of admiration has suddenly become a potential competitor. Even her current boyfriend starts looking at Virginie in a strange way. Pauline gets the feeling that Virginie is trying to pick him up.

After Virginie loses twelve kilos (22.5 lbs.), Pauline and Virginie fall out. Virginie's distraught. She doesn't know what's going on. Between her increasingly worried parents who are practically force feeding her, her best friend who isn't speaking to her and all the boys flocking around her, she feels completely lost. It's like she's become a different person. She no longer recognises herself. Even Hugo, one of her childhood friends, is behaving differently around her. Even her teachers treat her differently. In the end she starts wondering whether she hadn't been better off before...

When you want to change to feel better and happier, you always imagine your friends and family (who are supposed to want us to be happy) will help us achieve our goals. We tell ourselves:

"My loved ones (spouse, friends, parents, children), who love me and want me to be happy, will be delighted to see me change. They'll always help me, accompany me and support me. They love me – that's how things work!"

Most people who decide to lose weight think this as well. They know that losing weight will be good for their health and state of mind. Logically, their friends and families should be delighted to see them in better health.

The trouble is, they're wrong. My experience in helping hundreds of people change their lives has shown that often the worst enemies of our personal development are friends and family.

Maybe you disagree? Maybe, you think I'm talking rubbish! That's completely normal, because it's the truth, and this truth goes against everything you believe. Yet it's true!

And it's something you need to prepare for if you want to succeed.

WHY MIGHT YOUR FRIENDS AND FAMILY NOT WANT YOU TO CHANGE?

① THEY MIGHT BE AFRAID OF HAVING TO CHANGE THEIR HABITS

You've decided to change, but your spouse, your children, your parents and friend, haven't. You've decided to eat fruits and vegetables at every meal because you know they're good for you. But you need to understand that your friends and family don't necessarily share this desire. They might even be afraid that you'll try and make them eat fruits and vegetables too. They might be worried you'll make them change their habits to achieve their goals.

And they are right to be concerned! Because in fact, if you want to achieve your goal, you not only need to change your habits but also those of the people around you. A host of psychological studies have shown that it is very difficult to behave differently to your friends or family for very long. This is called "peer pressure". It will be hard, in the long term, for you to eat fruits and vegetables if the people you eat with don't do too.

I'm not saying it's impossible. I'm saying that it requires considerable energy, so you need, if you want to achieve lasting success, to change the habits of the people surrounding us.

Your goal will therefore be to transform your habits but also the habits of the people around you, at least the ones you share most of your meals with. It's a huge challenge, but it's worth the effort.
You're doing it for you and for them.

② THEY MIGHT BE AFRAID OF THE CONSEQUENCES

Rosie, who refused to lose weight for fear of cheating on her husband

Rosie was 37 years old when she came to me for the first time. Rosie was a very pretty woman, very curvy and very plump. She wanted to lose 25 kg. In our first interview she explained that she'd already lost 25 kg (55 lbs.) three years previously, but that she'd put it all back on again. I asked her why she'd regained so much weight so quickly. Her answer surprised me. After losing weight, she had cheated on her husband. Now she was afraid of losing weight for fear of cheating on her husband again.

So what in fact happened?

Rosie had always been curvy. She wasn't really used to being an object of desire. Once she lost weight all

At the time Rosie had three young children. Desire had overcome guilt, the fear of losing the life she'd spent so long building with her husband. So she made the decision to put all the weight she'd lost back on. Being overweight now acted like a "protective barrier" protecting her from men, their desire and her own desire.

Rosie's case is not untypical: by losing weight and in effect becoming more attractive, you put things out of kilter. Many husbands and wives will do all they can to stop their partner losing weight, consciously or unconsciously, for fear of being cheated on. A physical transformation always has consequences. Our love ones are often, wrongly or rightly, afraid of such consequences so they need to be reassured. If they are to be supportive of our change, they need to be informed, reassured and involved.

Papy Louis

*My whole life, I loved and respected my grandfather
Louis more than anyone else.*

*He was 1.68 m tall (5.24 feet) and weighed 110 kg.
(242 lbs.). He looked like Obelix. He was full-cheeked,
with a round belly and laughing eyes. He was so fat
that he couldn't tie his own laces.*

*I know his obesity caused him a host of health
problems. I remember going with my mum and him
to the doctor and seeing them argue about his diet
and his weight.*

*But when I was little, I wouldn't have wanted a
skinny grandfather for anything in the world. For
me a grandfather should be fat, or rather jolly. His
fatness gave him an extraordinary charisma, an aura.
In my eyes, he was the best granddad in the world.*

*In my mind, that's what a kind and affectionate
granddad looked like. Think about how Father
Christmas is depicted. I even remember telling my
parents, when they discussed his obesity, that I
refused to let him lose weight.*

I think I'd have been afraid of him losing weight. I'd have been afraid of my granddad becoming a different person. I would have been afraid of not recognising him. If you need to lose a lot of weight, this is something your friends and family might be afraid of.

Our loved ones recognise us through different characteristics features: our height, our weight our figure, how fat we are, our odour, our expressions, the shape of our face etc. Obviously, by losing weight we change our look. We don't have the same figure, the same appearance. Even our face changes. A skinny face has a harder, more sculpted, more severe look. Even our expressions change when we lose weight, especially when we lose a lot of weight.

Losing weight often means becoming a different person to some extent. Particularly if the person changes the clothes they wear.

For our loved ones, this transformation can be extremely disturbing. This is why in many cases they can literally "stop us losing weight". It's clear that as a child, I was a hindrance to my grandfather's weight loss as he could see that my love and admiration for him was partly down to the charisma his weight gave him. If he had lost weight, I think I would have told him I preferred him when he was fat! Imagine hearing that from the mouth of your 4 or 5-year-old granddaughter.

HOW TO GET YOUR FRIENDS AND FAMILY ON SIDE

---

1 TELL THEM

I meet a lot of patients who say:

"I PREFER NOT TO MENTION IT BECAUSE PEOPLE WILL CRITICISE ME IF I FAIL".

This is the first mistake to avoid. If you really want to prepare for weight loss, you must first talk to your friends and family. You need to let them know.

Why? Because otherwise, they won't understand why you're eating less, or differently.

If they don't understand, they'll worry (which is fair), or misunderstand your behaviour.

I remember another patient who'd decided to lose weight. To lose weight quickly, he'd decided to go on a strict diet. When he did the household shopping he bought only vegetables instead of the sugary, fatty or salty food he usually bought. His wife took this as a criticism. She was offended at the thought that her husband wanted her to lose weight! She didn't speak to him for several days. If he'd just explained that it was for his benefit, he'd have avoided this little domestic.

Gérard's wife

Gérard runs a company with almost 1,000 employees specialising in construction and public works. He started work at 14 and is still working at over 67.

Gérard came to me about his excess weight, especially around the stomach. In his discussions with me, he revealed that he went home for lunch e lunchtime as he lived right next to his place of work. His wife cooked for him and his two sons, who also worked in the company. Every lunchtime they were met with tasty dishes cooked with love.

My wife's speciality, he confessed, is dessert. And then there are always one or two squares of chocolate (for Gérard, normally three or four) with coffee. And then, Gérard told me, his wife always kept a stock of cakes to treat the grand children when they came to visit and...they visited often. The trouble was that Gérard loved cakes, and was devouring them on the sly!

We went for weeks without results until the day his wife came to the consultation with him. I explained that she needed to stop making desserts for lunch and buying cakes for her grandchildren. It was essential for her husband's health and would be a good way of showing her love for him.

The more you involve your friends and family, the greater the chance of getting them on side and therefore succeeding, because someone who is participating and involved becomes an enabler. They will want to support you, accompany you, help you and motivate you. By asking your friends and family to help you, you're quite simply showing them that you love them. And this act of love should overcome all their fears, worries or resistance. They will feel they're playing an active role in your transformation, enabling them to adapt more swiftly.

Here are a few ways of involving your friends and family in changing your life:

- If one of your friends plays regular sport, ask him to help you take it up.
- If your spouse cooks with a lot of fat, sugar or salt, ask them to cook healthier food – remember, they're probably cooking like that because they think you like it.
- If you live with someone, ask your partner to remind you if you start eating to excess.
- If you have children, pretend your weight loss program is a game, once which involves helping mum and/or dad lose weight. In this game, there are challenges like "not eating sugary cereals for breakfast" (because mum and/or dad eat a whole bowl of it in front of the telly in the evening), or giving up chocolate spread

(because mum and/or dad eat three teaspoons of it before going to bed). Show them how important their support is. And when you succeed, they'll feel like they played their part. Nothing makes a child prouder than making their parents happy. You just have to make the "losing weight" game more fun than eating sweets! In any event, you should use this lifestyle change to also change their eating habits. You will be doing them a huge service, and they'll thank you for teaching them to eat well when they're adults.

- If you go for a meal with friends or family, make sure you explain what you're doing simply and honestly, so they can avoid cooking something too rich. At least they won't be offended when you refuse to eat something they've slaved for hours over a hot stove to make.

A tip for family meals

I've been watching what I eat for several years now. I know I have a tendency towards excess. I was overweight as a child. When I go to my parents for Sunday lunch, I always ask for a "light" meal. I've been saying the same thing for over ten years now. And I must admit they've never listened to me...

In the end I realised that my mum was cooking because she loved it, and there were too many cultural barriers preventing her from cooking differently. My mum grew up in the countryside at a time when everyone sat down to eat at midday, not leaving the table until seven PM after eating two entrées, two main courses, a cheese plate and a selection of desserts. Preparing a light dish for a family meal didn't come naturally to her. She would have felt she was letting her guests down.

I had to learn to adopt strategies to avoid eating too much during these meals. I found the best strategy was "food allergies": gluten, lactose, eggs, or vegetarianism.

If you're allergic, nobody's going to force you. This lets me avoid certain dishes. If your friends and family ignore your requests, say you're allergic to certain foods. This will avoid peer pressure and upsetting them.

❸ ACCEPT THE FACT THAT YOU MAY HAVE TO CUT SOME PEOPLE OUT

It may be that changing your eating habits puts a strain on some of your relationships, or even causes you to lose some of your friends. Food can bring us together but also drive us apart. Imagine your best friend is a "meat fiend" who loves spending his evenings eating and drinking, and you decide for the sake of your health and wellbeing not to live like this anymore. Do you really think you'll be able to see him as often as you used to? Of course not.

This is why so many people never manage to stop over eating or drinking alcohol. Quite simply, they're afraid of losing their friends. Friendship should be a way of celebrating differences. Unfortunately, in reality this is rarely the case.

I myself have had to cut out many of my childhood friends because they can't imagine spending an evening without drinking and eating to excess. This was no longer consistent with my values. I admit it was difficult and painful, but it was the price of my personal balance.

If your friends are like that, try and suggest meeting them in a different environment, suggest doing sport, going to the cinema, a concert or an exhibition. If this doesn't work then don't worry, accept the fact that you'll grow apart.

The important thing in life is above all to live in a way that suits your values and deepest aspirations.

WHAT (POTENTIALLY) YOUR FRIENDS AND FAMILY MIGHT THINK WHEN YOU DISCUSS LOSING WEIGHT WITH THEM

If she loses weight, she'll become super-hot, and she'll be surrounded by guys! I need to start working out again! (Spouse)

- If he loses weight he'll become super-hot and women will start trying to pick him up – can I really trust him? (Spouse)

- Now she's on a diet, what will we eat when she comes for Sunday lunch? (Mother in law)

- Weight loss = diet = deprivation. I don't think things will be much fun at home. (Spouse)

- Mum's decided to lose weight! She'll probably ban all my favourite cereals that she keeps bingeing on. (Child)

- The last time dad went on a diet, we had no sweets for almost six months. I couldn't bear it. (Child)

- If he weights 10kg (22 lb.) less, when we go out I'll look obese. And no more boozy sessions! (Best friend)

- If she loses ten kilos (22 lbs.), she could outshine me. She doesn't even realise her potential! (Best friend)

- I'm sure she'll stop eating my favourite meals. Goodbye lasagne, chips and a cheeky MacDonald's on Sunday evening! (Spouse)

- You'll never win contracts by inviting clients to a vegetarian restaurant and drinking water! (Boss)

TO SUCCEED IN YOUR PLANS, CHOOSE 3 SPONSORS

To properly prepare for your weight loss, start by choosing three sponsors. Sponsors are friends, family, spouses, colleagues, etc. who will play a central role in the success of your plans. Their role is to:

1 SUPPORT YOU

Whenever you have doubts or hit a low point, you can call them or pay them a visit for their support. They'll help you overcome the difficulties you are facing, give you advice and encourage you to persevere. This is why the sponsors you choose must all be extremely positive and optimistic people. They need to believe in you and your ability to achieve lasting weight loss.

② MOTIVATE YOU

An e-mail, a text, a phone call to ask how you're doing and motivate you – this is the role of a sponsor. Your sponsors are there to give you energy, encourage you and boost your self-confidence and determination. These are people who share your ambition. They want you to lose weight just as much as you, because they think that what's good for you is good for them. These are people who consider your happiness above everything all.

③ TELL YOU THE TRUTH

Sponsors are people who can tell you the truth. You trust them to tell you things you might not want to hear. They are also there to call you to order, to tell you when you're breaking the rules, to put you back on the straight and narrow. These are people who you've permitted to do this. In return you need to accept what they say and show yourself ready to listen to what they have to say.

④ BE YOUR PYGMALION

A Pygmalion is someone who believes in you and your capacity to achieve change. Your sponsors should be pygmalions. In other words, people who believe absolutely in your success and your capacity to overcome any obstacles. They're people who'll do sport with you and encourage you

When you're running at 2km/ h. They're people who'll come shopping with you and encourage you to try new clothes, to change, to make a positive transformation. And your first sponsor is me. I will support you. I will motivate you. I'll tell you things you might not want to hear. Because I believe in you. I believe in your capacity to lose weight and transform your life.

Now, think of 3 sponsors from your friends and family. If you can only think of two, don't worry. Call them. Discuss your plans. Read this section of the book to them so they understand what you expect of them.

Write the names of the sponsors you've chosen here:

Sponsor n°1: ....

Sponsor n°2: ....

Sponsor n°3: ....

ACTION N°2:
PREPARE YOURSELF MENTALLY

The second stage in preparing for your weight loss consists of mental preparation. You need to prepare for your weight loss. For this, together we will use several visualisation techniques. These techniques have been proven to be effective in the field of top level sport and business.

So start by setting a goal for the next three months.

☐ 2 kg   ☐ 4 kg   ☐ 6 kg   ☐ 8 kg   ☐ 10 kg   ☐ 12 kg

Now you have set your goal, you can visualise it.

A note on visualisation techniques

Visualisation techniques are powerful techniques used in psychology and coaching to reprogram your thinking and behaviour. The more seriously you take the visualisation techniques suggested in this book, the quicker you'll get results. Whenever you do the exercises, make sure you concentrate and visualise

Close your eyes and concentrate, and imagine what you'll look like once you achieve your goals. Take your time to properly visualise and really perceive the different situations that are described. The more you're able to create a clear and precise mental picture in your mind, the more your goal will be imprinted into your unconscious. Your unconscious mind will then work like a guided missile, guiding you and spontaneously suggesting the actions you need to take to succeed.

VISUALISE YOURSELF PHYSICALLY

1/ Visualise the size and shape of your thighs, buttocks, belly, chest, arms, neck and face.
2/ Try to visualise yourself in the greatest detail.
3/ You need to perfectly visualise what you'll look like when you've lost all that weight.
4/ Once you've perfectly visualised what you'll look like after losing all that weight, do the following exercise.

NOW FOCUS ON YOUR PERCEPTIONS

5/ Perceive your goal.
6/ To do this, concentrate on your perceptions.
7/ Start by perceiving the fat you're carrying now.
8/ Feel where it's located.
9/ Start with your face and then go down the neck.
10/ Then concentrate on your chest.
11/ Go down further and focus on your belly fat.
12/ Continue and focus on your hips.
13/ You should perfectly perceive what you need to lose and where to lose it from.
14/ Now imagine that this fat is melting.
15/ It's being burnt off and dissolved by your organism as if it had decided to shed it, as if your metabolism had suddenly accelerated and your brain had ordered it to clear out that useless and cumbersome fat.

It's as if there was a lever in your brain's control room you could pull to speed up your metabolism and destroy this useless material.

PERCEIVE THE BENEFITS OF TRANSFORMATION

16/ Perceive all the benefits of getting rid of this cumbersome material.
17/ Perceive the lightness of your body as if walking on the moon, with sixteen times less density.
18/ You are light.
19/ You walk at a brisk pace.
20/ You're more self-assured.
21/ You have self-confidence.
22/ You have a sense of ease.
23/ Everything's going well.

FOCUS ON THE ACTIONS TO BE TAKEN

24/ Now imagine the actions you have to take to achieve this result.
25/ Look at them as opportunities for the change that life offers you.
26/ Picture yourself eating different foods, at different times, in different surroundings.
27/ Imagine how your life could be different, how you could be more active and do more sport or exercise, for example.
28/ Imagine an activity that you enjoy, and let the desire to do it pervade you.

SO, YOU'RE READY!

You're on the starting blocks for this major lifestyle change, which is to have a different relationship with change, which also means a different relationship with others and yourself.

ACTION N°3:
SPRING CLEAN YOUR CUPBOARDS AND YOUR HEAD

Olivier's safe

One day I went to visit one of my patients. As an experiment I wanted to see how he actually lived. He suffered from food cravings and snacking which had made him gain almost 30 kg (66 lbs.).

To help him break the impasse, I suggested visiting his home to observe his day to day life. I needed to place myself in the surroundings of his apartment to understand why he was overweight.

Upon entering the modest apartment, he shared with his wife and two children, I saw a big refrigerator. It was right in front of the door and was the first thing you saw when you entered the apartment.

I opened it and discovered it was full of all sorts of food. It was totally rammed. Olivier gave me a slightly embarrassed look, and then explained he was afraid of running out, so he did regular shopping.

I visited his apartment and went to a room he used as a pantry which he called, not without humour, his safe. In this room, Olivier had installed a giant two-metre high freezer. This was also completely rammed.

Inside were meat and fish but also pizzas, fires, quiches and ice cream...

Right next to the freezer was a big old cupboard that I opened. This was also full of different food: tins of tuna, pasta, oils, cereal, but also huge quantities of cakes and biscuits. And there were always several packages of the same food.

Olivier explained that to save money, he bought as much food as possible on promotion. Often it was much cheaper to buy several packets in bulk, at least that's what he thought. All his purchases were stored here and... in the cellar.

He took me down to the cellar, where there was a second freezer and a second pantry. Both of these were completely full. All in all, this small family of four had food stocks for almost two months.

Olivier's story is striking. His excesses reveal a tendency we can all relate to, that of stockpiling a large amount of food in our homes.

WE DO WE STOCKPILE SO MUCH?

There are several reasons. Obviously, it depends on the person. It may be for fear of running out. Some families lived through war in previous generations and passed on to their children the need to stockpile food, just in case... More generally, people who stockpile large quantities of food are victims of advertising. Indeed, advertising uses sales techniques which encourage us to buy ever greater quantities of food. Put another way, these people are manipulated.

WHAT ARE THE CONSEQUENCES OF THIS?

consequences are clear. The more food you have in, the more you tend to eat. Especially if the fridge is right opposite the front door, so it's the first thing you think of when you get home. The more food you store in your cupboards, the greater the chance of putting on weight in the long term. The opposite is also true. The less food you have in your cupboards, the better your chance of losing weight. So, to lose weight, you need to get rid of all this cumbersome excess.

WHAT SHOULD YOU DO?

In effect you have two choices: The first is radical. It involves taking a large bin bag and throwing out everything you've stockpiled. Throw out everything that's fatty and sugary, and any processed food.

Here is a non-exhaustive list of what you should throw away immediately:

- Ready-made dishes, pizzas, quiches and other tarte flambés,
- Chocolate spread, chocolate bars,
- Cakes, crisps,
- Processed meat,
- Frozen fries, potatoes,
- Chocolate or sugary cereals from some of the major brands,
- Chocolate covered bars, cereal bars, biscuits,
- Ice creams.

But that's crazy, you tell yourself! All that money out the window! What a waste! Maybe your parents taught you never to throw food away! Today this habit has become outdated. In France these days, nobody is dying of hunger, but rather of eating too much! So the opposite is true — sound and healthy people know that you need to throw food away, especially when you've bought unhealthy foods. What's the point of storing all that poison?

Think of the money wasted as the price of your stupidity and the error of your ways. This money is the price of becoming aware, the price of having a healthy life, living to a ripe and healthy old age. What's more important? Living healthier to a ripe old age, seeing your children grow, enjoying life as long as possible, or a few hundred Euros you were stupid enough to spend on buying toxic food that clever advertising convinced you to fill your trolley with. Think about it.

And I don't recommend you give it away, because you shouldn't give people poison.

Do it!

Because if you do it, it means you've reached your decision.

Do it!

Because this means that you're committed to the process.

It's like a smoker throwing away a packet of cigarettes or even a whole carton of cigarettes.

If you can't bring yourself to do it, then no problem. You just have to stop doing the groceries until you've eaten everything in your cupboards, in your freezer and your pantry. Obviously while eating normally.

Like compulsive gamblers, ban yourself from the supermarket! Their doors are shut to you.

Choose one of the two options and make it happen. If you don't feel like it, put this book away and carry on as you were.

Once again, you don't adopt a healthy, balanced lifestyle by magic. It requires concrete action, and this action can demand hard work and sacrifices.

To help you out, read the storey on the next page: the true nature of supermarkets!

A WOLF IN SHEEP'S CLOTHING

A hungry wolf keeps lurking round a flock of sheep. But the shepherd is watching his flock so carefully that he can't get anywhere near it. One day, not far from the pasture, the wolf found a sheepskin that the shepherd had left behind. Delighted at this windfall, the wolf donned it over his fur and mingled with the flock. Nobody recognised it because everyone thought it was just another sheep.

At nightfall, the shepherd, who was very hungry, decided to slaughter an animal for his pot. From his hut, he saw a sheep slowly approaching. As the wolf's disguise was almost perfect, the shepherd assumed it was one of his sheep and clubbed it to death. So, the wolf's ingenuous idea ended up being its downfall

Ésope

THE TRUE FACE
OF SUPERMARKETS

Imagine you're about to do your groceries at a supermarket. Like every week, you've come to stock up. Usually you're a quick shopper. You have so many other things to do. You want to be quick. But strangely, this day things are different. You've decided to pay attention to what you see, hear, feel and perceive when doing your shopping. You've deactivated your auto-pilot. You're going to do your shopping mindfully, paying attention and reflecting on it.

When you enter the store, you immediately go to the fruit and veg section, where there are several promotions. They're offering 1 kg (2.2 lbs.) of strawberries for the price of a 500-gram (0.11 lb.) punnet. What a good deal, you tell yourself! You pick up the 1kg punnet of strawberries and carefully place it in your trolley, delighted at getting one of your favourite foods for such a bargain, especially now you're trying to eat a balanced diet. After all your nutritionist has advised you to eat more fruit.

But suddenly, halfway down the aisle, you stop. You think for a moment and you realise how stupid you're being. What will happen when you arrive home? You'll be faced with an unavoidable dilemma. Either you eat the whole 1 kg punnet of strawberries, which is huge, or you throw half away, because strawberries go off in less than a night. In fact you've saved nothing at all. You've just bought too much to eat. And even fruits can make you fat if you eat too many.

You return to the fruit and veg aisle. You carefully return the punnet and pick up a 500-gram punnet which is not on promotion. By doing this you are acting as a smart consumer with an eye to your health and dietary balance. When you buy food, what counts is not a good deal but rather choosing food that's good for your health in quantities that suit your actual needs.

You carry on shopping and enter the cake aisle. Around you, perfectly lined up, are hundreds of packets of cake. This creates a certain amount of pleasure, indeed excitement, to see so many treats in the same place. On the colourful boxes are little smiling characters, jolly little animals, colourful drawings, games, gifts... It reminds you of your childhood! Your head is full of advertising slogans heard a thousand times a day on the telly or radio. You're tempted...

You're about to put a box of cakes into your trolley when something suddenly springs to mind. And if all those lovely characters on boxes of cakes were suddenly not so nice, what then? What if they'd been created by unscrupulous advertising agencies to sell more? You look at all those tiny characters and you suddenly realise they don't look at all nice. Their happy smiles hide sharp teeth, all the better to eat you alive.

The truth is that these people are not interested in your wellbeing. They just want your money. And to achieve this they're ready to use all sorts of strategies. They're wolves in sheep's clothing, just like in Aesop's tale. They don't dream of making you happy and healthy. They want you to buy and eat more and more cakes, even if they're full of sugar and fat which will make you ill with serious conditions like diabetes, or cause heart attacks.

They're merely packaging poison. You take a box and read the label. You realise that the cake is mainly made of sugar, palm oil and a whole range of industrial additives which are bad for your health. You see the truth and realise you shouldn't eat it. It's like little red berries in the garden. They look tasty but they contain poison. You realise that this food will kill you. You decide not to eat it.

You continue shopping, paying attention to what everything contains. You discover that most of the food sold there contains huge amounts of sugar, fat, salt and additives. Even ham contains glucose syrup! You realise that 90% of food sold in a supermarket are slow, deadly poisons. You realise you don't need all that to eat well. In fact, 90% of this unhealthy food is completely useless.

You realise that the major brands that have made such a mark on naive old you (slogans, music, little smiling people) and supermarkets are accomplices in this attempted poisoning. You realise that nobody wishes you well here. They just want you money. They're constantly trying, with massive promotions, to convince you to eat more. You realise that these places are run by criminals. What else should we call them?

You decide to go to the supermarket as little as possible. It's a place you should rarely visit. It's like a drugstore which only sells chemical products and you don't feel like giving your money to people who wish you ill. You don't feel like making people who are willing to make you ill just to earn more and more money happy. So that's decided, once and for all – you'll only go to the supermarket when necessary. And you will be very careful with what you buy.

THOSE FAMOUS EPICUREANS!

The death of an epicurean

One day I was chatting with a friend. He was terribly sad because he'd just lost his father to a stroke a week before. His grandfather had also died of a stroke, so he was also worried about dying young from the same condition. I asked him about his father's lifestyle. He smiled and told me: "He was an epicurean!" He liked to drink, smoke and eat! He was a bon viveur." He smiled. "I inherited this love of life from him!" Although I didn't show it, I was terribly shocked by his words.

Over the next few days I went over this conversation in my mind. I was flabbergasted – I couldn't understand what "loving life" had to do with people whose behaviour could only lead to an early or painful death. It was inevitable that my friend's father would die young. Smoking a packet a day, drinking alcohol every day and often to excess, and eating too much could only have one outcome. How sad, and what a lack of understanding!

From my point of view, this man was anything but "a lover of life". If he'd really loved life, he'd have done anything to preserve it. He would have stopped smoking, stopped drinking alcohol and avoided red meat. This chat with my friend helped me understand something essential: the fact that far too many people in France today confuse eating and drinking too much with happiness. There is a terrible confusion between being an epicurean and the meaning of the phrase Carpe Diem.

Being an epicurean, someone who loves life, means making the most of all the nourishment food life offers us. It means seizing life by the horns. But "nourishment" does here not mean food. Life offers a host of pleasures: dreaming, running, dancing, playing, making love, listening to music, contemplating a landscape or a work of art, reading a good novel or watching a good film, walking in the forest, learning a foreign language etc. All these pleasures nourish the soul. But they aren't food.

True epicureans love all these pleasures, all this nourishment, because they live in the now. Being an epicurean may mean being a good consumer, but not of meat or wine. Being an epicurean means consuming all the nourishment that life offers, and this comes in many forms. If you understand that, you can find the inspiration to change your life and your relationship with food. If you want to eat less, start by finding other "nourishment" to consume.

Instead of eating a packet of biscuits, read some poetry. Instead of eating chocolate, go for a walk. Instead of having a glass of wine, let yourself be inspired and feel the pleasure of just living. You need to learn how to find other nourishment and other pleasures. In this way you can replace food with pleasures that allow for self-development and make us happy instead of sad and ill.

Before losing almost 30 kg, my life revolved around food. As soon as I got in from work I'd start on my dinner. I would cook a huge plate of pasta with gruyere, lardons and crème fraiche. Then I'd eat yoghurts and biscuits all evening. When my wife brought it up I'd get annoyed, telling her told her she understood nothing about my lifestyle – I wanted to enjoy life. On the weekend, when I went out with friends, we'd go to a restaurant and spend our evening eating and drinking.
At the time I couldn't imagine living any other way.

And then I learnt. I must admit it wasn't easy and not without its setbacks. I began by taking up sport again – after getting in from work I'd spend 30 minutes on an exercise bike. Then I installed a punch bag, because I'd enjoyed French boxing when I was younger. I stopped watching TV and organised trips to the theatre because I love Boulevard theatre. Then I started going for after-dinner walks. I would walk in a park, taking my time. I'd think or just empty my head. Each time I tried to focus on the positive, always marvelling at small things like birdsong. All these things may seem futile and unimportant. Yet I learnt that these are the things which nourish us the most. The more time passed, the more weight I lost. Above all, my cravings disappeared. My mind filled with other things to the point that I now longer thought about eating, and I could stop eating without having to fight temptation.

THE TECHNIQUES USED BY THE AGRI-FOOD INDUSTRY TO MAKE YOU BUY MORE AND MORE

The agro-food industry has the best experts in advertising and psychology on its books, to persuade you to consume more and more processed foods. As an example, here are some of the techniques they can use to convince you to buy more and more. By better understanding these techniques, you can protect yourself against them. Understanding the techniques they use to influence and manipulate you will allow you to better resist them.

1 OFFERING PROMOTIONS ON BULK PURCHASES

One of the agro-food industry's favourite techniques to get you to buy more is the mirage of savings by buying more. Hypermarket catalogues are full of these promises of bargains. What might seem interesting from an economic viewpoint is absolutely wrong from a dietary viewpoint, because what will happen? Quite simply you'll end up eating more!!! You'll end up eating huge amounts to use up everything you've bought.

It's not your appetite that guides what you eat but advertisements and promotions. The pleasure of getting a good deal replaces the pleasure of eating well and being in good health. Who would you prefer to be? A person who always has a good eye for a bargain but who'll die from type II diabetes at fifty-five or someone who spends more on their food but eats healthily and will live to a ripe and healthy old age. Who's the smartest of the two? Think about it carefully.

② ASSOCIATING PRODUCTS WITH EMOTIONS

Advertising is intended to make you dream: the perfect family, a happy couple, a fun group of friends etc. To manipulate us, advertising agencies associate food with people's dreams. They're as cunning as foxes, except in their tale the crow eats the whole cheese. For example, to create an association with their products, they use music etched in our memories, which recalls real emotions. The memory of a special evening with friends will therefore be sub-consciously linked to a make of pasta.

Remember this. A child is playing on the banks of a stream. He's having fun skimming stones. When watching these images on TV, accompanied by gentle flute music, the view is immediately plunged back into his childhood. Who didn't skim stones on a lake or river when they were little? While you are immersed in your memories, a voice talks and imprints in your mind the slogan which encourages you to consume this make of mass-produced sausage. It's pure psychological manipulation!

Another technique is used by a famous brand of toffee. It writes funny stories on the wrapping paper which are always fun to read with your friends. Sweets are therefore associated with fun times. Unfortunately, this sweet is disastrous for your health. How many cavities have been caused by it, and how many teeth cracked trying to chew it? Just one sweet has almost 35 calories, and a packet almost 100.

Some people may retort that people have free will. Advertising doesn't force anyone to eat. That's very true. Nobody's forced to buy and consume a product because you see an advert. But, advertising is particularly targeted at young children who lack the means of distinguishing between true and false and good from bad. Children are very easily influenced for the simple and good reason that they are trusting. It is very easy to mislead a child. Once this has been done, it's very difficult to go back.

❸ MAKING YOU BELIEVE THAT SOMETHING IS GOOD FOR YOUR HEALTH

This is the latest way advertising agencies have found to respond to consumers' legitimate aspirations to look after their health. So, they invented "light" foods. The problem is that these foods generally have nutritional qualities which are not always favourable to weight loss. So, in some cases it may be the case that levels of fat are higher in so-called light foods than conventional foods. Put another way, manufacturers replace sugar with fat.

Advertising agents don't only create new products which only pretend to be good for your health, they also lobby the authorities, doctors and nutritionists. Here I can remember certain promotional campaigns for dairy or cereal breakfast products. The problem is that dairy products aren't necessarily good for your health. As for cereals, while they can be useful, most of the time they're sold with a huge amount of added sugar.

More recently, manufacturers have entered the gluten-free food market. The agro-food industry has noticed that more and more people want to eat gluten-free food. So they started producing this type of food and to replace gluten, they use fatty and sugary ingredients. So-called gluten free processed food is often very bad for your health and weight. I myself have eaten it, and was flabbergasted when I read the label of a gluten-free cake to find the first ingredient was sugar!

THE TRUTH ABOUT FOOD

1 SUPERMARKETS ARE NOT YOUR FRIENDS

Supermarkets, hypermarkets and other food stores are, by their very nature, businesses. Their aim is to keep selling more to earn more money. The butcher, the cheese maker and the fishmonger aren't smiley and friendly to you because they're your friends. They're not thinking about your health or wellbeing, but money above all else. This is fair enough, because selling is how they make their crust. But don't be naïve! Don't waste your affections on them. This will let you choose what's good for you.

I often find my patients have a certain amount of affection for the supermarket they get their groceries from. It's somewhere they go to buy nice things. They've been going regularly for several years, and know the checkout assistant or sales person. This "affection" often leads them to buy more than they should. The consequence is pretty obvious: the more food you buy the more you eat. Doing your groceries therefore requires a certain amount of prudence.

② BIG BRANDS AREN'T INTERESTED IN YOUR HAPPINESS

Chocolate spread, chocolate bars, cereals…you see all these products perfectly packaged with depictions of nice, smiley people. Be aware that brands are just trying to manipulate you by putting those nice people on their packaging and trying to create an affective relationship with you. Once of my best friends, a floor manager in a big supermarket, recently told me how angry some customers would get when the store was out of their usual brands.

Be very wary of this affective relationship with brands, particularly those you've known since childhood. These big brands are definitely not interested in your happiness. They're just trying to manipulate you to sell more. What sometimes alarms me is when I see much-loved brands that are partly responsible for the death of thousands of people a year from obesity and weight-related illnesses. It's reminiscent of the affective relationship created by cigarette manufacturers between tobacco, a deadly poison, and smokers.

③ TELEVISION ISN'T THERE TO ENTERTAIN US

Lastly you need to understand one final thing. Television isn't there to entertain us but to attract your attention to sell you stuff you don't need. Have you ever wondered why so many cooking programs have appeared over the last few years? Because the public love cooking programs? Of course not! These programs have been created with the sole aim of selling advertising spots to the major agro-food brands.

This is why great chefs have become stars! It's the agro-food industry that's behind these programs. It's merely a more pernicious type of advertising. If you want to lose weight and live to a ripe old age, I heartily recommend you either stop watching TV or watch it with both eyes open. And above all stop watching programs dedicated to food. Their only goal is to get you to eat, and eat badly.

Because what happens after watching an expert pastry chef or even a skilled amateur create delicious, succulent pastries? Of course you feel hungry! As you are unable, and will probably never be able, to create such pastries, you go and buy them from a supermarket. This is no good for your weight or your health, as mass produced pastries are full of chemical additives without real nutritional qualities beyond their excess sugar and fat.

SUPERMARKETS ARE NOT CHEAPER

In 2016, a journalist from Le Figaro newspaper conducted an experiment on the cost of foods purchased in supermarkets and hypermarkets, comparing then with the cost of food bought from local food networks, such as organic basket schemes or foods bought directly from producers. The journalist tried them both for two months in a row. Here are his conclusions. They're surprising, and challenge received wisdom about supermarkets:

"In one month I spent 264.50 Euros on all my day-to-day consumer needs: cosmetics, household products and foods. The previous month I'd spent 300 Euros at the supermarket alone".

In short, by using local food networks, this journalist saved almost 10% on his monthly shop, so this experiment challenges a commonly held belief. A second study carried out by the Paniers Marseillais association came up with the same results: organic fruits and vegetables marketed through local networks are cheaper than supermarkets. Another result: fruits and vegetables sold in an organic basket are on average 29% cheaper than in a hypermarket.

WHY ARE SUPERMARKETS MORE EXPENSIVE THAN LOCAL NETWORKS?

FEWER INTERMEDIARIES

A local network involves direct sales from the producer to the consumer, limiting the number of intermediaries. According to the Intelligence unit for the formation of price and food product margins, out of every 100 Euros spent on food in supermarkets, 37.6 Euros goes to the supermarkets, 13.2 Euros to the agro-food industry and 8.2 Euros to farmers. By reducing intermediaries, you reduce costs and therefore reduce the cost of food accordingly. Eating well also means eating more cheaply.

LESS WASTE

Also, when they sell directly, producers offer "imperfect" fruits and vegetables. A gnarled vegetable will sell as easily as a perfectly formed one, which in turn reduces losses. For customers, waste is also reduced. Using local networks, customers are less tempted by unnecessary purchases, and consume more responsibly. Eating better therefore means helping to preserve our planet by fighting waste. It means helping to preserve resources while making savings.

10 PRECONCEPTIONS ABOUT DIET

1 "TO LOSE WEIGHT YOU NEED TO CUT OUT DESSERTS"

Fruit and dairy products are important food groups and should be eaten at each meal. In terms of cakes and other desserts, you can treat yourself from time to time as long as the rest of the meal isn't too heavy and starchy.

2 "SKIPPING A MEAL HELPS YOU LOSE WEIGHT"

When you skip a meal, your body stores the energy it needs in reserve, but will then store more to replace it.

This method is therefore counter-productive – it's better to eat little than completely skip a meal.

③ "CHEWING GUM REDUCES HUNGER"

Chewing gum might temporarily reduce your desire to eat, and can replace snacking. However, chewing causes salivation, which risks stimulating your appetite.

④ "YOU SHOULDN'T DRINK WHILE YOU EAT"

You often hear that drinking too much during a meal can lead to bloating or stomach pain. But water actually has the opposite effect, as it encourages digestion and the elimination of waste.

⑤ "FRUIT JUICES ARE LESS SUGARY THAN FIZZY DRINKS"

Most fruit juices are as sugary as fizzy drinks, sometimes more. The best drink to quench your thirst is obviously water. Juices and sodas should be dropped from your diet, at least when you're trying to lose weight.

⑥ "YOU NEED TO EAT MORE WHEN IT'S COLD"

We often feel like eating heavier meals in the winter, but our bodies don't expend any more energy in winter.

On the contrary, to protect you from the cold and keep your body temperature at 37°C, your body tends to store more in winter than summer.

⑦ "A SANDWICH ISN'T A BALANCED MEAL"

You can have a balanced diet even if you haven't got the time to cook. For example, by choosing a protein rich food (meat, fish, eggs), raw vegetables and a piece of fruit, you can create a balanced meal.

⑧ "FROZEN VEGETABLES LOSE THEIR VITAMINS AND MINERALS"

Most frozen vegetables contain as many vitamins and minerals as fresh vegetables. Indeed, generally the time between being picked and being frozen is so short that they keep their initial properties.

⑨ "LIGHT PRODUCTS HELP YOU LOSE WEIGHT"

Just eating light products is not enough to achieve any real weight loss. An effective diet is essentially a matter of quantities. We are mainly interested in the proportions of each food group in your diet.

⑩ "STRICT DIETS ARE EFFECTIVE"

Strict diets involve excluding certain types of food from your diet to force the body to dig deep into its resources to melt fat. They are known for their rapid results but are generally ineffective in the long term and cause "yoyo" effects.

OUR ADVICE WHEN GOING SHOPPING

BUY AND EAT AS LITTLE PROCESSED FOOD AS POSSIBLE!

YOU WILL LOSE WEIGHT AND LIVE LONGER

STAGE 3:
UNDERSTANDING YOUR EXCESS WEIGHT AND WHAT YOU NEED TO DO TO LOSE IT

WHY ARE YOU EATING TOO MUCH AND POORLY?

Why do we eat? The simple and obvious answer is: because we need it to live. The problem is that this response is inadequate. It's a cold, scientific and biological response. Thinking that people eat only to allow their bodies, their brain, bones and muscles to function is reductive. Because in reality, that's not the only reason people eat. Otherwise we'd only eat a paste containing the right amount of nutrients, like in some science fiction film.

Eating is an activity which in reality encompasses a host of facets.

Firstly, people eat differently depending where on earth they live. People living in France, the United States or China don't eat at the same time of day, or the same foods. I've travelled a lot and eaten foie gras in France, liquid meals in San Francisco and live fish (before I became a vegetarian) in Japan. Eating is a social activity which has its origins in the culture and tradition of each country, each family, and each person.

And then eating is also intimately linked to our relationships with others. The first exchange a child has with another human is an exchange of food with his mother. Even in the mother's stomach, the symbiosis between the mother and her baby is linked to the provision of nutrients. More than facial expressions or touch, this is the first way two living beings interact. Eating has a social but above all affective dimension. By eating or feeding someone else, we give and receive love.

Finally, eating is linked to our identity. If I tell you: this person eats rice for lunch and dinner every day, you'll probably assume this person is of Asian origin. If I tell you they mainly eat hamburgers, you'll think they're American. What we eat and when we eat says something about who we are. It defines our identity. And then eating changes our appearance. We don't attribute the same personality traits to a very skinny person as a curvy person!

If you want to lose weight and adopt a healthier and more balanced lifestyle, you need to consider the affective, emotional, relational, social and identity-based dimensions of food.

This is what we're going to do now.

In the next few pages you'll finally understand why you eat too much and what you can do to change.

Over to you!

REASON NO. 1:
YOU EAT TOO MUCH AND POORLY BECAUSE YOU NEED LOVE IN YOUR LIFE

Anna's life

Anna came to me as part of the Psy'Action® program. This program, conducted in our practice, consists of 5 sessions with a nutritional dietician, and aims to restore dietary balance over 5 sessions with a psychologist (me).

She wanted to lose 8 kg (17.6 lbs.) The dietician gave me a picture of a woman focused on weight loss, quite anxious indeed sad and uncomfortable in her skin.

Anna was a maid. She worked for several demanding clients. She earned about 800 Euros/ month, and still lived in the family home with her mother, now very elderly. She rarely went out and had no friends. She never travelled or went on holiday; she had no children, no partner, and didn't want one.

What I was immediately struck by was her surprising emotional existence. Who hugs her, listens to her, gives her affection? I sensed a certain emotional drought, like a sponge that hadn't seen water in a long time.

Other than her mother, who seemed to be a very kind woman, and brothers and sisters, who occasionally invited her to lunch, she was alone. There was however one person who seemed interested in her wellbeing – a young girl called Emilie, who she'd nannied. For Emilie, she said, with a glint in her eyes, she was a bit like a second mother.

Anna would lose over 10 kg (22 lbs.) on this program. To achieve this, in addition to the dietary support provided by Valériane, the nutritional dietician, I would help her do three things: the first would be to reconnect with this young girl who loved her so much.

After making contact, the young girl, who'd recently moved to Morocco to run a travel agency, invited Anna to spend a week's holiday with her. On her return, I discovered an Anna transformed, surprisingly lively and overflowing with happiness. For someone on their own, love is like water to someone crossing the desert.

Next we would work on her relationship with her mother, who she also loved greatly. Anna just needed to be more aware of it. Finally, Anna learnt to love herself. To achieve this I suggested different exercises. And throughout the program we would also give her a lot of love.

Why do we eat too often and too much? Why do we suffer from food cravings? In some cases, these cravings are linked to a lack of love. From the day we're born, we associate eating with being comforted, cuddled and loved, simply because this is the first thing our mother did for us. Eating and being loved are inseparable activities. Years later, when we feel the need to be comforted, cuddled, loved, we can try and satisfy these needs by eating.

This is typical with heartbroken people who compensate with chocolate, people stressed by their work who, as soon as they get home, binge on cakes or buttery toast, or eat too much in their evening meal. Yet this should be a light meal because the body consumes less energy during the night, so excess calories are automatically stored in the form of fat. The most common reason for overeating is therefore a need for love.

To lose excess pounds, you need to start by satisfying this unmet need.

Obviously you can't force others to love you. So what to do? Basically you need to do something extraordinary, something surprising but relatively easy: just learn to love yourself. If you really love yourself, you'll become a stronger and more independent person. You'll develop self-confidence. By loving yourself you'll make other people want to love you, and easily overcome your weight problems by satisfying this need to be loved.

But how can you learn to love yourself? Don't worry.

You just need to learn.

WHAT IS LOVE?

I have a personal and very precise definition of love. For me, love is the sincere desire to see another person grow, develop and improve. Put another way, love is the sincere desire to see another person live! Because what's life other than this constant intention to grow, develop and improve? Is this not what all living species, plants, animals and human beings, have in common? Plants want to grow, animals seek to reproduce and human beings want to improve.

Love is a feeling we can ascribe to any living being. It's certainly not restricted to Man, let alone our family circle. I must admit to experiencing feelings of love for my patients. When I meet a patient, I immediately experience the desire to see them make a positive change. This is an urge I feel at the heart of my being. I want to see them live! I want them to get their spark back, see them move.

When I talk about lacking love, I'm simply saying we're missing out on relationships with people who feel this towards us. But remember, you can be surrounded by people and not receive love. I recall a young woman called Betty, who lived on a farm with by her husband, her three children and her parents in law. She was surrounded by people but was suffering because none of them really loved her. Nobody wanted to see her realise her own potential, evolve and grow.

Loving means wanting the other person to evolve in a way that suits them, and accepting this. It means respecting their freedom. So a parent can have feelings for their children without really loving them. This could be the case if they try and force a career on them or make them behave in a way that doesn't suit them. The child won't feel truly loved. He will just feel manipulated. And no doubt he'll manifest the symptoms of this lack of love, which can range from depression to unhappiness, over-nutrition or obesity.

It's also possible to lack love if you're in a relationship if your partner fails to see you as someone who is evolving, and doesn't support this change with motivating and encouraging words. You can also lack love from your children if they're incapable of seeing you as anything more than a mother or father who isn't evolving. And it's the same thing at work, if our manager doesn't believe in our capacity to evolve, improve ourselves and become better people. In this case, we run the risk of losing our spark.

I've been working as a therapist for almost 15 years now in different fields (work, family, couples, health, etc.), and I've reached the conclusion that all the patients who come to me with symptoms of unhappiness are in fact lacking love. And this is precisely what these same patients are seeking in my practice, and what they find: people who love them, simply because we have a sincere belief in their capacity for positive change.

In terms of diet, the impact of a lack of quality relationships with others regularly translates into excessive weight gain. By eating, people try to reconnect with their primitive experience in childhood with their parents. By eating, they're trying to rediscover the comfort they experienced during the first few months of life when their parents would nourish them with a heartfelt desire to see them live and grow. People are seeking love.

The trouble is that these attempts are in vain because consuming food in itself does not provide love. It lacks an essential ingredient: someone who loves! But people nevertheless compulsively repeat the same behaviour without perceiving the truth. Food cravings are linked to this type of conditioning and illusion. For example, excessive consumption of biscuits is often just an attempt to rediscover the positive emotions felt when you were a child, when snacking.

Food cravings and over eating can only, in these cases be combated by developing new, quality relationships with loving people in the here and now. Once again, it's not necessarily a case of finding a partner. You can find love in your relationships with your friends, our children or parents, but also in your relationships with your colleagues, clients or patients. The important thing is that these people want us to develop and grow.

By building quality relationships, people will discover a psychological and physiological balance that will regulate their appetite as well as the storage of fat, reducing weight gain or enabling weight loss, without any extra effort. When you achieve this, you don't even think about eating excessive quantities. On the contrary, when you feel loved, when you love yourself, you merely feel the desire to care for yourself by eating a balanced diet in reasonable quantities.

EXPERT SCIENTIFIC OPINION ON THE LINK BETWEEN FOOD AND LOVE

Oxytocin is a hormone produced by the hypothalamus at key moments in life like giving birth, the first few months of a child's life, human relationships and social relationships in general. Oxytocin is called the "attachment hormone" because it's produced when people are in contact with people who love them. This explains why we suffer when separated from people who love us. We're lacking this hormone. Oxytocin is the hormone of love.

Recent studies have shown that Oxytocin acts as an appetite regulator, particularly among obese men. A team of German researchers conducted an experiment on a group of men. At the end of their meal they were offered chocolate biscuits.

Results varied depending on whether or not the men had received a dose of oxytocin (by nasal spray): it turned out that the men who'd received a dose of oxytocin consumed 25% fewer biscuits than the men who hadn't. The same experiment was conducted with some young people. In this case, no difference in behaviour between the two people was noted.

The German researchers concluded that oxytocin blocked the desire to "eat for pleasure" and not "true" hunger. Eating when you're not hungry could therefore be linked to a lack of oxytocin, a lack caused by situations of social stress or the absence of positive and fulfilling affective relations.

Another study was conducted on mice. Several studies had already shown that mice that were lacking Oxytocin could develop obesity without their diet changing. Among obese mice, other studies had shown that injections of oxytocin enabled a reduction in weight gain. During this study, over almost 2 months, mice were put on a fatty diet before receiving intracerebral injections of oxytocin for two weeks. This enabled a 50% reduction in weight gain by these mice without any change in diet.

Oxytocin, or the love hormone, therefore plays a key role in weight gain. By stimulating the production of oxytocin, we can thus influence the appetite and storage of fats in the body. The more you love, and the more you feel loved, the more of this hormone you'll produce, and the more your desire to eat when you don't really need to will reduce. You'll only eat more when your body tells you to because it needs more nutrients.

EXERCISE: LOVING YOURSELF

A note on visualisation techniques

Visualisation techniques are powerful techniques used in psychology and coaching to reprogram your thinking and behaviour. The more seriously you take the visualisation techniques suggested in this book, the quicker you'll get results. Whenever you do the exercises, make sure you concentrate and visualise things as precisely as possible. At first, you might find it a bit difficult, but by persevering the images will appear and you'll see the effects. To develop your capacity to visualise, do the following exercise before doing the exercise suggested in the book:

- *Visualise a colour in your mind. Think of a colour that evokes pleasant memories/ sensations for you.*
- *Then think of a sound. It could be a piece of music or just a simple sound that evokes pleasant memories/ sensations for you.*
- *Then think of a smell. Recall a smell that evokes pleasant memories/ sensations for you.*
- *Then think of a taste, the taste of a good or anything else that evokes pleasant sensations/ memories for you.*

We can't ask others to love us. Firstly because they don't necessarily know how to do this, and also because it needs considerable time and energy, which, depending on their situation, they might not be capable of. And finally because in some cases they simply don't feel like it. But there's at least one person on this earth who can provide you with strong, constant and unconditional love – you.

• • •

I want you to think about someone you've loved with all your heart, someone you've experienced profound love for. They might be your children, your parents, a spouse, a friend, a teacher or someone else.

I want you to think very hard of someone you've loved with all your heart. You loved them profoundly and sincerely because you wanted this person, more than anything, to live, grow, develop and become a better person.

You profoundly and sincerely wanted this person to be healthy and happy in their personal and professional life.

You wanted this person to be happy. This feeling of love filled you almost to overflowing.

I'd like you to profoundly consider this feeling of love. I'd like you to really feel it. Keep thinking about this person, really think of them, concentrating on your feelings towards them: this profound desire to see them develop, grow, live...This profound, complete and sincere desire to see them happy each day of their life.

And feel this profound feeling of love pervade you. This feeling fills you up. It fills you up like a bath with hot water. You feel a warmth grow in you, and this warmth is the love you feel for this person; this profound and sincere feeling, this powerful feeling of seeing them develop, going from strength to strength, achieving all their goals and dreams. You experience this feeling growing in you, you are focused on this person. You're focused on the love you feel for them, and this love fills you completely.

Repeat in your mind:

"I love them, I love them, I love them".

And each time you say these words, you experience the love you feel for that person grow.

"I love them, I love them, I love them".

And each time you say these words, you experience the love you feel for that person grow. This love is like a mighty river flowing into the sea. The sea is the person you are focusing all your love on.

• • •

And now, gently, you divert some of this flow to yourself. You direct some of this love to yourself, towards your body, your spirit. Your love is focused on this person but also yourself. You feel the same feeling for them as for yourself. You feel the same desire to see yourself evolve, expand, grow and be happy every day of your life.

You want to make your life a success with all your heart. You have a profound desire to feel good, to be in good health, to respect your body and mind. You have a profound desire to achieve your goals and realise your dreams. You believe in yourself. And you feel all the love you felt for this person instantly flow towards you. This love envelopes you and runs through you. It's like wrapping yourself in a blanket, a blanket which warms and protects you.

You feel a profound and sincere love, a powerful and constant love for yourself, a love which gives you energy and reassures you. It's strange, it's gentle, it's warm, it's light. This love is a powerful feeling of wellbeing and compassion for yourself.

It's like a balm that eases pain, of the body and soul; it's like a balm that sooths all the problems and scars of life. And you spread this balm over all that affects you. You spread it over all your thoughts and all parts of your body. And when this balm comes into contact with your mind or body, you feel its healing energy. You feel wellbeing replace pain. You feel peace of mind replace anxiety. You feel serenity replace fear.

You feel so good. You're there, connected with yourself. You're bathing in the waters of your own love.

And now you know that you can experience love for yourself. And now you know that you love yourself profoundly. And you understand what it means to be loved. And you swear to love yourself sincerely and profoundly from now on.

Make an oath to yourself. Tell yourself: from this day forward I swear to love myself profoundly, sincerely and unconditionally, whatever the situation and whatever happens.
If you agree to take this oath, clench your fist.

. . .

From this day forward, you will take the time to love yourself. You'll take the time to feel this energy pervade you, heal your injuries, ease your pain and give you energy, a powerful, gentle, constant and eternal power of love for yourself, this profound desire you have to expand, to grow, to develop and progress, all the important things in life.
That's it, you love yourself!

This is an extraordinary feeling because you discover that you don't need other people to achieve it. You can love yourself if you want because you need only create this love for yourself for it to exist. This makes you a free and strong person. And you can now, because you truly love yourself, love others.

And because you love yourself, there's nothing else you really need. You're completely satisfied, replete, complete. You've found what you were missing. You're complete, whole.

You're like a jug brimming with water, like a stream in springtime, like the sky full of summer sunshine, like a bright full moon. And you feel completely replete.
Feel this sense of fulfilment.

An extraordinary discovery

I don't think I really learnt what love is until I was 35. From the moment I understood what love was, I understood its true strength. Love is normally seen as a sentiment, but not in this case. Outside the realm of relationships between partners or family members, we avoid using it, or do so with a certain reluctance, especially if we're male. When I started using this word I felt embarrassed, uncomfortable. And then I became accustomed to using it in my work because no other words describe the attitude you need to adopt with yourself and others if you want to achieve happiness. There are no other words to describe love's true power of transformation. Because if you love yourself you'll be able to transform yourself, and if you love others you'll help them change. There's no resistance to change unless there's an absence of love.

REASON N°2: YOU EAT TOO MUCH AND POORLY BECAUSE YOU'RE STRESSED OR ANXIOUS

One of the main causes of malnutrition is stress. Stress is a biological reaction of the body in the face of external or internal attacks. This could be heat or cold or an overly intense physical or mental activity. Stress is also caused by inter-personal contacts, time pressure and the lack of resources to face a problem. Our society constantly asks more and more of us in less time and with fewer resources. This is why we're stressed!

Stress is obviously not without its consequences on the body. A body under stress is like a car engine pushed into the red. This "overload" exhausts the body and causes both physical and psychological problems. Stress and anxiety are two evils that can soon reduce a person's quality of life and their physical and psychological health. Symptoms are numerous and affect every organ in the body (see diagram).

I used to be very stressed. I had to run regular conferences and training sessions for the elderly, and in the weeks leading up to these events I was under huge amounts of stress. This stress manifested itself in joint pains, bruxism (I used to grind my teeth at night) and severe pains in the back of my neck and my back. Also, I kept falling ill, with colds or bad chests.

As I got older I learnt to manage this stress, particularly through meditation and self-hypnosis (which I will discuss in this chapter). These techniques helped me reduce my stress levels by almost 80%. I immediately saw and felt the difference. My life had changed! I only rarely fell ill, I had no more neck or back pain. I stopped grinding my teeth and my joint pains had become much less frequent and intense. It also had a huge impact on my diet.

Now I will explain how reducing your stress will help you lose 10 kg and live 10 years longer.
Let's do it!

THE SYMPTOMS OF STRESS

At a physical level:

- **Skin:** more sensitive to illness, slower to heal,
- **Brain:** problems with concentration, mood and sleeping,
- **Bones & muscles:** fragile bones, muscle cramps and contractions, tendinitis,
- **Immune system:** decline in immune defences, allergies,
- **Cardio-vascular:** tachycardia, hypertension, heart attacks,
- **Digestive system:** ulcers, constipation, haemorrhoids,
- **Sex drive:** drop in libido, impotence, amenorrhea.

<u>At a psychological level:</u>

- **Moods:** aggressiveness, affective lability, sudden mood swings,
- **A decline in cognitive capacity:** difficulties concentrating, memory loss, decline in reasoning capacities,
- **Behavioural problems:** agitation, feverishness, inhibition, inability to reach to events, feelings of being unable to take the initiative.

THE EFFECTS OF STRESS ON YOUR DIET

- How does stress affect our diet?
- How does stress make us eat greater quantities of unhealthy food?
- How does stress make us gain weight, and does it reduce our ability to deal with day to day challenges?

Here's the explanation:

Stress puts the body in a state of urgency. A person under stress is always in a rush. Their brain has decided, wrongly or rightly, to mobilise all of its available resources to deal with a situation it sees as threatening or dangerous. The most common problem is stress at work. People have to mobilise all their resources to confront the problems and challenges they encounter at work. That's all they think about. That's where all their energy goes.

① STRESS MAKES YOU EAT JUNK FOOD

A stressed person spends as little time as possible eating. For example they'll spend fewer than ten minutes on lunch so they can get back to work more quickly. Skimping on lunch means you eat more quickly. This means they'll often choose ready-made dishes: sandwiches, pizzas, hamburgers, etc. They'll be tempted by fast food or fatty and sugary processed foods (even in savoury processed food, manufacturers add sugar in the form of glucose syrup).

② STRESS MAKES YOU EAT TOO QUICKLY

Stress also puts people in a dissociative state. They become fixated on their personal and professional concerns. They forget everything else. They eat quickly without thinking about what they eat because their mind is elsewhere. So they ignore their body when it tells them it's full and tend to eat more. Studies shown that you only become sated after a certain amount of time. If you eat too quickly, you won't feel sated and will eat too much.

③ STRESS NEEDS TO BE COMPENSATED

Malaise caused by stress makes a person seek to mask and compensate pain with pleasure. It's impossible to bear a state of chronic stress without compensating for it somehow. Fatty and sugary foods create gustatory pleasure which masks pain and general malaise. Obviously this "mask" soon slips. So you need to keep on eating. This is why stressed people tend to snack, something which can turn into bulimia.

I remember a recent experience of mine. After a difficult and stressful day at work, after getting home I went to do my groceries. I wanted to observe my reflexes. Normally I limit myself to fresh fruits but after that stressful day

I wanted to "treat myself". Also I bought a whole bar of chocolate, which I devoured that same evening. If I'd had bought cakes I would probably been tempted to eat them too. Fortunately my cupboards were empty!

When I come home from work feeling fine, I want to make this feeling of well-being last by eating healthy, balanced food. I don't buy cakes, chocolates or sweets because I know the pleasure they bring is temporary compared with the problems they cause. The digestive problems they cause last for hours, and can even be felt in the morning. When you eat too much of such food, you get a type of "food hangover".

If you want to lose weight and live to a ripe and healthy old age, you need to reduce your daily stress levels. For this you need an action plan. Having myself suffered from a lot of stress, I've tried various solutions. The advice I give here is far from exhaustive. It's up to you to find your own path. The important thing is to make reducing your stress levels a priority. The more you reduce your stress and anxiety levels, the easier it will be to eat healthily and in the right amounts.

TIPS FOR REDUCING STRESS BEFORE, DURING AND AFTER MEALS

① BEFORE MEALS: REDUCE PRESSURE

Reducing your stress levels before a meal is vital if you want to avoid the three phenomena we identified above: (1) Eating Junk Food; (2) Eating too much (3) Eating fatty and sugary foods. For this you need to create certain rituals. This means that you carry out a ritual before each meal. A ritual is a series of actions you repeat each time which allow your brain to identify the shift from one state to another. This is the ritual we suggest adopting.

When you get home in the evening, start by changing into comfortable clothes. Keeping the same habits means keeping the same mental attitude. You will get more of a feeling of having left work and fewer responsibilities when you're wearing pyjamas! Put your computers and smartphones away – it's time to relax. To relax even more try putting on music which evokes a sense of relaxation and brings back pleasant memories. What about the music you listened to on your holiday?

Next, hop on your exercise bike. You should do between 15 and 30 minutes of cycling. If you get bored on the bike, make the most of your time by watching a conference online, or playing a game that relaxes you. If you don't have an exercise bike, you can go for a walk. If you can't, or don't want to go for a walk, get an exercise bike. It costs a hundred Euros and lets you do sport at home come rain, snow or wind. You'll have no more excuses not to do the right thing.

Finally, take a shower to completely relax. Exercise has allowed your body to get rid of the adrenaline flowing in your blood. Adrenaline is produced by stress, and unless you get rid of it, it will continue to act several hours after being produced. Showering lets you wash away the toxins that have accumulated on your skin, particularly if you work or live in a polluted area. In Paris, when you wash you face at the end of the day, it's not uncommon to find grey much in your handkerchief.

If you want to relax even more, why not do some yoga or stretching? Obviously all this takes time. If you are stressed, you might well say you simply don't have the time. Make this time! If you want to spend time with your children, why not do yoga with them! As for your exercise bike, there's nothing to stop you putting it in the middle of the lounge so you can be in the thick of things.

Some rituals you can perform before eating your evening meal:

- Play with your children or take them to the park,
- Play your favourite musical instrument,
- Make love,
- Have a foot or leg massage,
- Go swimming,
- Listen to music,
- Meditate,
- Do the gardening,
- Walk home,
- Cook.

DURING MEALS

It's important to reduce stress factors during meals. One thing you should absolutely avoid while eating is watching the news, as news programs essentially focus on dramatic or tragic events that cause the body stress. We will discuss this in another chapter, but watching TV can also bring about a dissociative state. Put another way, you don't think about what you eat, so you can end up eating anything to excess.

It's also important to avoid conflict, whether with your spouse or family members. Meals should be a sacred moment where conflicts are not permitted, and if conflicts cannot be avoided, it's better to eat alone. Meals should, as far as possible, be a time of pleasure and conviviality. What could be nicer than this chance to nourish your body, allowing you to be healthy and live a long life? Eating is a form of self-care.

Things you should stop doing:

- Eating in front of the news – you can watch the TV as long as it's a good comedy.
- Eating while checking or playing with your smartphone – it's important to be mindful while eating,
- Eating while arguing with your spouse or children

If there are tensions between you and your partner or children, eat alone.

AFTER MEALS

Pavlov's dogs

You may be aware of Pavlov's famous experiment. Pavlov was a doctor who studied the behaviour of dogs. He set up a small experiment. Each day before feeding his dogs, he would ring a little bell. He repeated this for several weeks until his dogs had associated the sound of the bell with meal times. After that, when he rang the bell his dogs would salivate even if they weren't being fed. The bell had become the signal that they were going to eat. This experiment teaches us a lot about the way the brain and body operate. They need signals to react. At the end of the meal, you need to give your brain and body a signal that you've finished eating. Why not a little bell which rings and means: that's it! It's over.

In the past, people would do the washing up after meals. Now we all have dishwashers. So there are no more rituals as such after meals. The disappearance of these rituals is damaging in the sense that, in the absence of any rituals, your brain finds it hard to realise the meal is over. Consciously you know, but sub-consciously the brain doesn't really know the difference. So you need to do something, always the same thing, which means "there, that's it! I'm not going to eat any more today."

Here are a few examples of rituals than can help you signal the end of the meal:

- Doing the washing up,
- Drinking a herbal tea, tea or coffee,
- Going for a walk,
- Cleaning your teeth,
- Chewing gum (sugar free),
- Reading the newspaper,
- Listening to a piece of music,
- Meditating,
- Doing the gardening,
- Reading a chapter of your favourite book.

TWO TECHNIQUES WHICH CAN HELP YOU MANAGE STRESS AND ANXIETY

1 HYPNOSIS

Before I learnt hypnosis at Pitié Salpêtrière Hospital in Paris, I was an anxious and stressed person. My young age compared with my level of responsibility meant I was in a permanent state of stress. By training in hypnosis I learnt techniques that helped me relax and reduce my stress levels. On a scale from 1 to 10, I'd say I used to have a stress level of 8, and now I'm between 1 and 2 depending on the situation.

Going to see a hypnotherapist can help you reduce your stress for good. In addition to getting common sense advice and healthy living practices, you should manage to reduce your stress and anxiety levels and therefore achieve a state of wellbeing. You can then do self-hypnosis, a technique close to meditation. This technique brings about a state of relaxation and letting go. There is a whole range of self-hypnosis sessions to listen to online and the main online video sites.

② MEDITATION

Meditation is a technique which allows you to either empty your mind or focus on a subject sufficiently to allow the mind to "forget" the elements which are causing you stress. In a state of stress, the mind focuses on your personal and professional concerns. By managing to clear your mind or teach it to focus on other subjects, you'll teach it to relax and allow your body to reduce its levels of stress and anxiety. Meditation is therefore a powerful tool for reducing stress and anxiety.

There is a whole range of meditation sessions to listen to online and the main online video sites. You can also take courses organised by meditation groups or teachers. As it's a new practice, it may take some time to learn at first. But it's really worth the effort – the benefits of this technique are excellent for your physical and mental health. You will develop your concentration capacity and your memory.

TAKE SOME TIME
FOR YOURSELF

Stress is like elastic

Imagine you're holding a piece of elastic between your fingers. Stretch the elastic by spreading your fingers and feel the tension of the elastic between your fingers. Now you understand what stress is. Stress is the tension between what you have to do, on the one hand, and the resources you have to do it on the other.

You have only 24h a day to sleep, work and look after your children, spouse and yourself. You have a million and one things to do, and only a certain number of hours in the day. Of course, the more you have to do, the faster you have to do it. Stress increases!

Some of my patients who come to me to lose weight can be surprised when I suggest they change their habits. Initially they don't realise that having a stressful life places them in a situation of psychological imbalance that they often fix with an excess of fatty and sugary foods.

To lose weight, you often need to start by loosening the elastic, in other words reducing stress levels. This means you need to make a choice when it comes to your day to day activities. You need to get rid of activities that create the most stress and introduce relaxing activities into your life that will help you loosen up.

You need to develop your capacity to make choices, and that means giving some things up. You can't do everything. Some activities should be eliminated from your day, while others should be delegated. For example you could hire a cleaning lady or delegate some jobs to your family members to reduce your housework.

And this means developing your ability to say "No". For example if you're stressed at work, you need to be able to say "No" to your boss, your colleagues or customers. This will avoid you taking work home with you.

Knowing how to say "No", politely but firmly, is the beginning of self-affirmation.
Finally, you also need to learn to say "No" to yourself. We all want to live our lives to the max: activities, experiences, opportunities... But this can also lead to taking on too much, causing burn-out. Bear in mind that the best way of making the most of life is above all to live a long, healthy life.

Be the tortoise not the hare. That's the beginning of wisdom!

OUR DAY TO DAY ACTIVITIES

In this table, write down your most important day to day activities. Ideally, create a table for your personal and professional life: Then, in the columns on the left, note down whether you plan to keep this activity, because it's essential, if you're getting rid of it or delegating it. For example, in your work life, a task may be delegated to a colleague or employee. In your personal life, if you have the funds, you could get a contractor in to prune your trees or mow your lawn.

WHAT I DO	I KEEP	I GET RID OF	I DELEGATE

Finally, add the fun and relaxing activities you would like to add to your work and personal life:

118			

EXPERT SCIENTIFIC OPINION ON THE LINK BETWEEN FOOD AND STRESS

Dozens of scientific studies have been conducted which establish a link between stress and being overweight. One of the most interesting shows that people on a diet tend to eat more in stressful situations. To lose weight, people control their diet. They need to pay more attention, which requires more energy. The trouble is, stress can also place a heavy burden on their energy reserves. In a stressful situation, these persons can suddenly lose any control over their diet, which results in massive and uncontrolled binging. This is why stressed and anxious people are more susceptible to bulimia (Greeno & Wing, 1994).

Conversely, people who don't attempt to control their diet because they are in tune with their body are much less sensitive to stress, and in stressful situations they generally don't eat any more than usual. Several studies have shown that people on a diet tend to eat more in response to stress, while those who aren't watching their diet eat less (Lattimore & Caswell, 2004; Polivy & Herman, 1999). Put another way, if you're in tune with your body, you will be less sensitive to stress. Quite the contrary, stress will make you eat less. We will discuss this subject in the chapter on listening to your body's hunger and appetite signals.

An important study conducted in Finland showed that the BMI (measurement of weight-size ratio) is higher among people subject to stress, and that they generally consume more fatty or sugary foods like sausages, hamburgers, chocolate and pizzas than other people (Laitinen & Sovio, 2002). People subject to stress find it harder to control their eating. Their attempts to lose weight are ruined by stress, which makes them consume large amounts of fatty or sugary foods. Put another way, if you're stressed and try to go on a diet, there's every chance of you putting on weight! Stress and diets are an explosive cocktail when it comes to putting on weight!

8 FOODS TO FIGHT STRESS

To fight stress, nothing is better than healthy living. This means doing physical exercise and adopting a balanced diet. Some foods have qualities recognised to help you reduce stress and anxiety. The effects of these foods have been proven – they help you fight anxiety and stress thanks to the nutrients they contain and act on the very nature of the hormones and neurotransmitters produced by the body. Let's look at some of these stress-busting foods now!

① OILY FISH

Oily fish are rich in <u>omega-3</u>. They therefore help reduce anxiety. But make sure you don't eat farmed fish because they are full of heavy metals. Choose wild fish instead. Also consider rapeseed oil, which is the richest oil in Omega-3. It's the healthy oil par excellence!

② CAMOMILE

Camomile is a traditional remedy against stress and anxiety. It won't perform miracles, but it will help you improve your mood and get to sleep easier. Also, drinking herbal tea in the evening will help you hydrate. It's an excellent ritual for finishing off your meal.

③ ALMONDS

Almonds are very rich in zinc, iron and fatty acids. They are a good supplement to a balanced diet. Thanks to their iron levels, they combat brain fatigue, which can cause a loss of energy and anxiety. Eat them before your meal, like an aperitif, for example, a diet aperitif!

④ GREEN TEA

Tea helps reduce anxiety. Make drinking tea a habit by following a ritual. Use a teapot and share it with your colleagues, friends or family members. These few minutes will allow you to relax and reap the benefits of theanine, an amino acid which has known for its calming effects.

⑤ WHOLE WHEAT PASTA

Whole what pasta is highly effective against stress and anxiety due to its high levels of magnesium and tryptophanese. These elements are actually precursors to serotonin, the happiness hormone. As they are filling, whole foods also help fight hunger, which can cause anxiety.

⑥ SEAWEED

In the West, we generally don't eat much seaweed. Yet it is rich in nutrients, magnesium and trytophanes, and is a good alternative for people who are gluten intolerant. Over the last few years, Spirulina has become very fashionable. It's an excellent algae for your health. Try it!

⑦ PROBIOTICS

Some studies have shown that bacteria in intestines can either encourage or avoid obesity. It has also been found that eating processed foods changes the very nature of these bacteria. Probiotics that can help you rebalance your intestinal flora are on sale in pharmacies.

8 BLUEBERRIES

Since I started eating them every day I've stopped getting ill. Blueberry belongs to the super-food category. They are rich in both vitamins and anti-oxidants, known for their anti-stress and anti-anxiety properties, meaning they give a lasting boost to your immune system.

REASON N°3:
YOU NEED TO BE FREE

The boy who wanted to be free

My parents would buy cakes just once a week, on Friday evenings. They would never buy sweets, chocolates, ice cream or fizzy drinks… My parents never drank alcohol, or at least only rarely. They would eat simple dishes, often prepared using raw foods. From October to April we had soup every evening.

For a long time I felt my parents didn't know the meaning of pleasure. I must admit to sometimes being jealous of other kids who had cupboards full of cakes and chocolate, and a freezer full of vanilla and chocolate ice cream. I dreamt of having a mum who would make me fries!

Later, as a teenager, I started drinking alcohol. At that age I found my parents boring. I told them they didn't know how to enjoy themselves – they never cut loose. I even ended up finding them strange. I didn't want to live like them. I told myself: I want a life of pleasure! I wanted to be an Epicurean.

The year I graduated from school, I went to study in another city. Finally I had my own apartment. I could eat and drink what I wanted when I wanted. Right away I set to eating fatty and sugary food: each morning I would buy pain au chocolat, and each evening I would eat fries, pasta or pizzas, with cake for dessert.

So eating for me had a subconscious meaning I was unaware of. Because what I was enjoying at the same time as the pain au chocolat, cakes, fries and pizzas, was my freedom. That freedom I had waited for so long. I was savouring the ability to live a different life to my parents. I could live MY life.

As I'm very tall and did several hours of sport a week I didn't put on weight despite this very unbalanced and unhealthy diet.

Of course, as I got older I couldn't continue with these bad habits that were destroying my health. But I found it really difficult. I found it really hard to stop eating all these harmful foods. Subconsciously, it felt like going backwards and losing my freedom. It meant living like my parents.

Then one day something clicked and I understood. If you want to lose weight, you need to understand it too. Food, and particularly alcohol, has nothing to do with Happiness. True Epicureans know that to make the most of life you must first preserve it. Life is fragile and needs to be cared for. A happy life is a healthy and long life. It took me 15 years to understand that.

I then understood that my parents weren't living a boring life but a simple and healthy one. I understood that I had been wrong to look forward to eating those unhealthy foods for so many years. I understood that eating these foods had nothing to do with freedom or happiness. It was just an illusion.

① ABOVE ALL, BEING FREE MEANS NO LONGER BEING UNDER THE INFLUENCE

Some of my patients refuse to make lasting changes to their eating habits. They say: I want to be free to eat what I want! I want to drink hot chocolate if I fancy it, or eat a pastry. And they say: I also want to be able to have a drink before dinner and eat crackers. In their mind, cutting out certain foods and drinks (despite being toxic) meant restricting themselves, limiting their freedom. Eating fatty and sugary food was a symbol of freedom.

Listening to them I realised how successful the marketing men had been. They had managed, thanks to television and magazines, to make thousands of people believe that eating ice creams, crisps and cakes and drinking fizzy drinks was freedom! They had conditioned us to associate food with freedom. Marketing men are true magicians. They could convince us that black is white. It took me a long time to realise their deception.

As the marketing men would have us believe, on the one hand are serious, boring and unhappy people who eat fruits and greens. Their life is drab. They don't know how to have fun. Conviviality is a foreign word to them. They don't know what it means to enjoy themselves. On the other hand are people who live an intense and exciting life, the cool people. These people have fun. They have loads of friends, eat ice creams, pizzas and fries and go to fast food restaurants. On the one hand is a life of frustration and on the other a life of pleasure.

People who choose to eat foods that bring about so-called pleasure are in fact not "choosing" anything. They are under the influence. They are under the yoke of industrial groups worth billions of dollars, which make them believe that by eating such and such a food, they will be happier. They are not free, quite the contrary. They aren't deciding a thing. All they're doing is blindly following what they're told in adverts. Others decide for them: brands, supermarkets, the agro-food industry, everyone who has an interest in them filling their stomach.

My daughter is 4. Like many young girls she's a fan of the film the Snow Queen. She loves that cartoon. In supermarkets, you never images of the Snow Queen on salads but on processed food packaging, and this attracts her attention: she wants to eat all those foods. She's already being manipulated by shameless marketing men who manipulate her little heart to make her want to eat junk food.

And we've all been there. You've been there. Once you were a child who trusted and believed what people said. A child who believed that by eating those cereals you'd become the most popular kid at school, or by eating those sweets you'd get super powers and fight off the baddies. We've all been manipulated to think that choosing to east these toxic foods is a type of freedom. I drink fizzy drinks, so I'm the coolest person on earth!

That's patently absurd!

❷ BEING FREE MEANS REDUCING YOUR DEPENDENCIES

Being free does not mean choosing between two brands of cola, it means being able to drink a large glass of water, which won't make you dependent on caffeine and sugar. Someone who is happy with a simple glass of water to quench their thirst is the freest person on earth. They need nothing to make them feel good, so they can feel good wherever they go. Being free means knowing how to behave differently to everyone else. If you decide to be different, then you are really free.

When I ate too much ad my body showed its displeasure through reactions and ailments, I told myself: "Why can't I eat that?" That's unfair." I blamed my own body for being unable to digest all the food I was eating. I ended up almost hating it. I felt like I had been singled out, thinking everyone else could eat large amounts of ice creams, pizzas, sweets and cakes without ever falling ill.

In fact I was wrong, because I realised that most people make themselves ill with the food they eat. But they refuse to open their eyes to the fact that it's due to food. They attribute it to "illnesses" and visit the doctor to cure these illnesses or conditions. This is the case, for example, with GERD (gastroesophageal reflux disease), which I suffer from like almost 1 in 3 French people. I have read a great deal of literature on this "Illness". Most people take medication to fight it; others even undergo fruitless operations.

Why? Quite simply because GERD is not an illness. There is nothing doctors can do against this condition. At the very best they can mitigate its symptoms, because GERD is linked to diet, the fact of eating too much fatty or sugary food, particularly in the evening. People who suffer from it are like me. They don't think it's normal not to be able to drink this or that food. They think it must be linked to an illness instead of thinking that it's eating too much fatty food that's abnormal.

The human body is not designed to digest processed food. It is not designed to assimilate such large amounts of food containing so much fat and sugar, not to mention the additives and other chemical elements added to food. The human body is not fragile. It's processed food which is toxic, which is why so many people fall ill from over nutrition and malnutrition. The problem is that after several years, illnesses, suddenly very real, develop.

❸ BEING FREE MEANS MAKING A FUNDAMENTAL CHOICE

We need to recognise that we don't really choose what we eat. We are born in a certain country at a certain time, into a certain social circle. It's our culture which defines what we should eat. Evidence of this is that we don't all eat the same foods, whether we're in France, the United States, China or Japan. Our diet is totally determined by our education. This is true until the day arrives when we question what we find on our plate and decide what's really good for us.

Because the mere fact that our culture, our parents or our school have taught us to eat certain foods over others says nothing about their intrinsic qualities and their capacity to ensure a healthy and ripe old age. Put another way: It's not because it's normal to eat certain foods that they're good for our health and balance. Just because everyone else eats a food doesn't mean we should, let alone because advertising tells us to.

In France, tradition tells us to eat white bread. But is white bread (or even wholemeal bread) really good for us? In the same way, we are strongly encouraged to consume dairy products. But is cow's milk really good for us? It is really necessary to eat it when they don't in other developed countries, yet live long, healthy lives. Finally, we are encouraged to eat meat. But is it really good for us to eat meat?

I'm not here to tell you to stop eating bread and meat or stop drinking milk (even if I personally have stopped consuming them). I would just say that if you want to be free, really free, you should stop, for at least a while, whether a few days or a few weeks, considering it normal to eat these foods, giving you the opportunity to profoundly change your diet. It's by giving yourself this possibility that you can change.

Because it's clear that these modern foods are no good for our health. Otherwise, why would 46% of people in France be overweight? Some will claim that the figures are exaggerated, that it's the diktat of thinness. After being 340 kg overweight, and experiencing the torment caused by the over consumption of processed foods, I can't let that stand. It's a fact – these days we eat too much and eat poorly, and that makes us sick.

If you really want to be free, give yourself the time, something I feel is really necessary, to question your diet and lifestyle. You need to give yourself time to explore and discover new foods, new ways of cooking, new ways of eating. In short, you need to get out of a rut and do things in full knowledge of the facts, so you can then decide what's good for you. Experts will always disagree. Only your opinion counts.

Just a few months ago I was totally convinced I was eating healthily. I was stuck in a rut. By becoming more flexible in my way of thinking and behaving, I gave myself permission to explore. So I rediscovered the pleasure of eating certain vegetables. I started eating loads of fruit, transforming my diet. And this gave me enormous pleasure. I found it hugely liberating.
Now it's your turn!

WHO ARE THE TRUE REBELS?

In the media these days you often see complaints that we're living in a world dominated by the Diktat of thinness, and that there's social pressure on people to be thin. The media generally "force us" to be thin so we should rebel against this pressure, accept and vaunt the virtues of being curvy. I believe those who think that are wrong – I think it's exactly the opposite. The pressure is to eat too much and eat poorly.

You really want to be free. You really want to take back the power over your life. In this case, find the strength to say NO. Clench your fist and say NO. No to the television which floods you with cooking programs just to sell adverts for food. NO to the fact that food is often a substitute for interpersonal relationships. NO to barbecues, NO to cookies, NO to crisps, NO to cola and NO to chocolate spread!

Recently, while attending a fair, I discovered a magazine dedicated to health. This magazine used to be called Belle Santé (Good Health) but the publishers of the magazine recently decided to change the title to Rebelle Santé (Health Rebel). I thought this title was great because it perfectly expresses what you'll become by changing your lifestyle to lose weight and live a long, healthy life. You'll become a rebel. True rebels are not punks or hippies—just people who adopt a healthy lifestyle.

Now that's cool!

EXERCISE: EXPERIENCE TRUE FREEDOM

Imagine you weigh 10 kg (22 lbs.) less. Feel the lightness running through your whole body. Imagine how fast you'd be able to get around. Imagine you can run or walk quickly. You're not walking, you're flying. You're as light as air, and a world of possibilities is now open to you. You can get to places you couldn't before. You can walk for longer, see and discover more things. You can go further than you ever did before.

Now imagine you can do sport, that you can go out dancing. Imagine all the time you used to waste by eating and collapsing on your sofa because your body was using all its energy to digest. Imagine all this time now becoming a huge free space you can fill with leisure activities, fun, meetings and discoveries. You can also leave it empty to become a time of relaxation and wellbeing.

You don't see food like you used to; you no longer see cola, crisps, hamburgers and processed meats like you did. You don't see it as a pleasure but a millstone, a heavy millstone stopping you from getting on your feet, a millstone slowing you down and preventing you from realising your dreams and desires. If you've got too fat, it's because they want you to stay fat. Colas, fizzy drinks, sugar, pastries, processed meats and cheese are not foods, they're prison bars.

Imagine you're in that prison. Feel the walls closing in. Feel that sensation of losing your freedom. See how those bars keep you locked up. And then push the door open. Leave that prison. Indifference is key. Let yourself be indifferent. Feel how free you can become by leaving all those toxic foods on the roadside. And suddenly you feel totally free, light as a feather. You're like an astronaut on a rocket ship to the stars.

The bars fall away, and life spreads before you like a vast land to be conquered. So many things to learn, people to meat, adventures to experience. Maybe, at the moment, you feel that is all very far away. Maybe you feel content with your partner, work or family. You just need to dream. Because food is just an illusion, something which keeps you looking at your feet, when there's a whole world open to you.

CHOOSE WHAT MAKES YOU FEEL GOOD

I remember my first ever sip of beer. At first I thought it was horrible! It was bitter, and more than anything just made me want to go to the toilet. Then, over time, the more I drank, because my friends and I felt it was a vital part of becoming an adult, I started to enjoy it. From hating it I grew to love it. I drank much too much for years, until I decided not to touch another drop.

And we can reproduce this example with other foods. It's a fact – to love a food you need to get used to it. In reality, the psychology of taste means we love what we're used to eating. This means we don't love a food for itself, but rather we learn to love it. Understanding this opens up huge possibilities of transformation and change, meaning that in reality, we can choose one food over another.

So when providing dietary support in our practice, I see patients move from a real addiction to a food like chocolate to a state of total indifference to it, and sometimes even disgust. Patients are often surprised to discover that they can choose what emotion to ascribe to food. They often wrongly believe that they have no influence over what they feel about food but this is completely possible. It's all psychology.

Today I'm simply unable to go and eat a hamburger at a fast food restaurant. I'm so disgusted by this type of food that I'm physically unable, yet a few months ago, I would willingly go there to eat on Sunday evening. How did I achieve this? Simply by force of will and psychology exercises. I'll give you some examples of such exercises later in the book. If you think about it, it's not surprising that it works, because it had to happen the other way when we were growing up.

By discovering this possibility, patients discover a new sense of freedom. So they can profoundly change their diet by learning to love new foods – good foods – while giving up the food of the past – bad food. It's a quite surprising and fun game. The first way of exercising this freedom is therefore to play with your beliefs and adapt them to suit you. Imagine you could be as excited at the thought of a cucumber as a bar of chocolate!

7 CULTURAL DIFFERENCES WHEN IT COMES TO FOOD

By force of habit we tend to think the way we eat is universal. Let's look at the differences between France and other countries when it comes to eating. This will help you open your mind to new things and try new ways of eating.

1 MORNING, MIDDAY AND EVENING

The first time I went to the Ukraine, we had lunch at 4.30. In that country, eating is seen as a functional activity. You eat to live, you don't live to eat, and above all you only eat when you're hungry. If you're not hungry at midday, you don't eat – you wait until you're hungry before going to a restaurant. We got up from the table at five thirty. I found that strange at first, but then I understood that it wasn't so strange to eat only when you're hungry.

2 EATING FOR PLEASURE

In France, eating is associated with pleasure. On a trip to San Francisco, in companies in Silicon Valley I discovered a new way of eating – instead of having lunch in their company canteen, employees stayed at their desk and drank a drink containing all the nutrients necessary for a balanced diet. Goodbye traditional cuisine, hello functional eating. It seemed strange at first, and then I realised that in the end there's more to life than eating.

③ STARTER, MAIN COURSE, DESSERT

If you ever go to China, you'll find that during meals they put everything on the table: sweet and savoury, the starters and the main course. In fact these concepts don't even exist. You can eat "dessert" before your "starter" and the "main course" before your "starter". Only in France do we have such a regimented approach to food. This should make us think, because often you end up eating a dessert when it's not necessary.

④ EATING MEAT

Buddhists don't eat meat yet they don't lack for proteins. Proteins are necessary to develop muscle mass, so they're mainly useful for highly active people. Today, most of us spend our days in front of a computer. Our need for protein is therefore much less and largely met by other sources of proteins – starches and dairy products. Meat is therefore unnecessary.

⑤ EATING WHEAT

Wheat is the staple cereal in Europe. In South America it's corn, while in Asia it's rice. So this can give you an idea of how to diversify your diet by adding new cereals or even plants like Quinoa and buckwheat, which are great for your health and rich in protein. Generally we eat too much wheat, particularly processed wheat, where the most gluten-rich varieties have been selected, which explains the growth in gluten intolerance.

⑥ DRINKING ALCOHOL

Buddhists don't drink it, and neither do Muslims but it doesn't stop them from celebrating and being happy. When I was fourteen, I attended a wedding in Morocco and we spent the evening dancing, singing and laughing like I never have with alcohol. There were musicians and a great energy. In France, it seems inconceivable to imagine a wedding without alcohol. Yet celebrating without alcohol is much healthier.

⑦ EATING CHEESE

The French eat more cheese than anyone. In Asia, eating a piece of Roquefort is like eating a scorpion for a French person. We may love eating cheese, but a diet without cheese is still a balanced one. The same with yoghurt! Remember, if you're encouraged to consume dairy products, it's also because the dairy industry is so powerful. Many people consume no cow's milk without suffering from ill health.

STAGE 4:
RECONNECTING YOUR BODY AND MIND

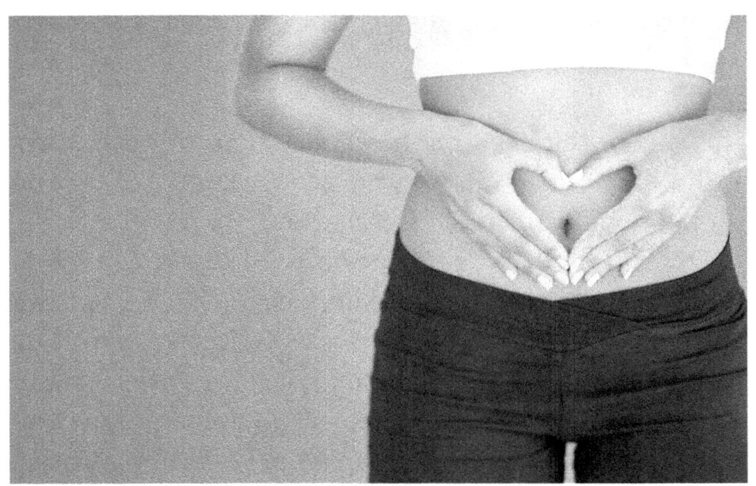

RECONNECT YOUR BODY AND MIND

The society we live in has severed the unique link between body and mind. This has its origin in religion, which sets the pure and noble soul against the vile and soiled body, a separation which was then taken up by philosophers of the enlightenment who differentiated between reason, qualified as pure and noble, and intuition, instinct and senses. Enlightenment philosophers invited people to mistrust their senses. This distinction carried over into industrial and post-industrial society which organised itself around it.

This way of thinking that has developed over centuries, and which we have become accustomed to, can be summarised as follows: On the one hand is the body, which is low, which feels but does not think. The body is the place of instincts and impulses. This part of the human being needs to be mastered and controlled; otherwise humans will be no more than animals. On the other hand is the mind, which is the noble part of the human being. The mind is capable of elevation through reasoning which leads to truth and wisdom.

Western societies have organised themselves around this separation between body and mind. Professions, for example, are divided according to this way of thinking. Medicine deals with the body and psychology the mind.

This is why, in traditional dietary advice, the psychological dimension is more of an afterthought, despite being central, and despite the fact that it's not really possible to distinguish between the two. The body is in the mind and the mind is in the body. We are a single entity.

This distinction has caused society to elevate the mind over the body. The world we live in pays no respect to biological rhythms and human activities these days do not respect the body. They even constantly try to go beyond its limits. In this respect the world we live in is totally inhuman, because it is adapted only to a part of ourselves. It is designed to satisfy our mind and not our body, which has other needs and expectations to function properly.

Here are a few examples:

- The time you have to get up in the winter to study or go to work is the same as in summer, yet biological rhythms linked to exposure to light are very different. We get up at the same time whether we're a child, an adult or OAP, despite the fact that waking and sleeping rhythms differ depending on age.
- The human body is designed to move. It's necessary to alternate between periods of physical effort and rest. However, most professions these days are sedentary ones. We hardly move at all. The arrival of television in our homes only made us more sedentary.
- In our personal and professional lives, we plan more and more. Plans are projections into the future and are not suited to the body, which needs immediacy. The body is the place of action and the present par

excellence. It needs to be "here and now" to function properly.

- Meal times are defined by our education. We don't eat when we're hungry but according to the opening hours of restaurants and mealtimes allowed at work or school. We have to eat 3 meals a day even though the body may have different needs.
- More and more people suffer from stress. Stress consists of permanently exceeding your physical and mental capacities. Stressed people don't listen to the signs of fatigue given off by their body. They don't rest. They focus only on mental aspects.
- The amount of food we eat exceeds the body's capacity to assimilate. The human body gives off signals. But rather than acting on them, we interpret these natural limits as illnesses. We try and mask symptoms with medication.

The man who wanted a brain transplant

One day, one of my patients, who was over 50 kg (110 lbs.) overweight and suffering physically because of this excess weight, told me with a tear in his eye that if it were possible, he'd like to transplant his brain into a robot. He wanted to become pure mind. His body was causing him so much suffering that he wanted to get rid of it.

He didn't realise that his suffering was because he was totally disconnected from his body. He spent his time working in front of a computer. A "computer engineer" by training, he developed programs and algorithms that he designed at home for companies based around the world.

He could spend fifteen hours completely disconnected from his body, completely absorbed with his intellectual activity. Of course, when he stopped working and returned to reality, he ached all over. He'd spent fifteen hours sat in the same position on a chair, his eyes fixed to his computer screen.

His body had sent him various signals of discomfort (eye strain, backache, cramps) but rather than heeding these signals, he merely focused more on what he was doing. By remaining focused on his work, he had stopped noticing his discomfort, until he returned to reality. And that was extremely painful.

And that's why he ate too much. He was ignoring the signals from his body. When I asked him when he had last eaten because he was hungry, he admitted that it had been several years. He ate almost permanently, despite some serious digestive problems.

EXERCISE:
EAT ONLY WHEN YOU'RE HUNGRY

The first stage in reconnecting your body and mind is to eat only when you're hungry. Often we only eat according to the rules, which set fixed mealtimes and what we eat. For example, we eat in the morning right after we wake up because experts tell us we need a hearty breakfast in the morning. Since our childhood we've become accustomed to listening to experts and conducting ourselves accordingly. We also do it because it's more practical to eat at home, except...

Except eating just after you wake up isn't really necessary! It depends on the time you ate the night before, how much, and your physical activity in the evening or overnight. If you ate a light meal at 6 o' clock and made love all night, you'll definitely be starving when you wake up. But if you had a large meal at 8 o' clock and all you did is sleep, you're probably not going to be hungry, quite simply because you don't need to eat.

Generally, rhythms imposed from outside cause us to mistreat our body.

Always doing the same thing

Personally, over the course of a week I end up getting up at different times. When I go to my Paris practice I get a very early train and get up around 5, but when I work at my local practice I get up around 8. I realised that whatever time I got up, I always had breakfast right afterwards. I also realised that on the days I got up very early I would suffer from digestive problems. They were minor issues I would ignore, blaming them on the fear of missing the train, but in the end I realised that the problem was not stress but the fact of eating when I wasn't hungry. My digestive system was still asleep at 5 in the morning, and was in no mood to deal with another influx of food. I would often eat automatically, without thinking and without listening to my body. Now I've changed my habits my digestive problems have disappeared. It's made a clear improvement to my quality of life and fitness levels on the days I need to work a long day and cope with several hours commuting.

Let's take another example – lunch. All the experts agree that this should be the second largest meal of the day. Personally, I realised that if I ate too much for lunch, I felt like taking a nap until four in the noon. But taking a nap was incompatible with my work. So should I listen to the experts and force myself to eat, even though I'm not hungry at midday. In the evening, on the other hand, I'm really hungry because I'm relaxed. But the experts tell us it's wrong to eat in the evening.

I think that when it comes to food, your body is the best expert. Everyone needs to find their balance according to what they feel. Rather than reading a pile of books on food, you're better of learning to identify the signals your body sends you when it's hungry and ready to receive food. Only eat when you're hungry. Wait until your hear your stomach rumble. Let it feel empty. Really feel the sensation of hunger. This is the first stage in reconnecting with your body. I've personally experienced this reconnection, and these are some of the benefits I got from it:

- Better digestion with a significant reduction in digestive problems (GERD, heartburn, constipation),
- Greater pleasure in eating, and becoming much more sensitive to taste (when you're hungry, it's as if the body is more sensitive),
- A reduction in the amount of food I eat during the day, with no more snacking.
- While learning to understand signs of hunger is vital, it's also a good idea to learn to recognise the signs of being full. When you eat, there comes a time when your body tells you:

"THAT'S IT, I'M FINE, I'M FULL!"

Obviously if, like many people from my generation, your parents told you to always clear your plate, you won't listen to the signs of being sated, and will force yourself to eat until you've cleared your plate.

So you clear you plate even if you get stomach ache for a couple of hours afterwards.

To properly feel when you are sated, you need to take the time to eat in such a way that your body can produce enough hormones to indicate you are full. To achieve this, take a break between the different courses. Avoid scoffing the starter, main course, desert and coffee straight after each other like stressed people do. Pay attention to the feelings coming from your stomach. You should not feel too full.

To summarise, do this exercise for a week:

- **Only eat when you're hungry:** You should wait until you're really hungry before sitting down at the table. This means not having breakfast if you're not hungry when you get up. You shouldn't eat robotically or by habit, but according to what your body tells you. It's not your mind but rather your body which decides, because it knows what's best for you – it's the expert. It's up to you to learn to speak its language.
- **Stop eating when you're no longer hungry:** as soon as you feel a slight tension in your stomach, stop eating and move on to something else. If you pay attention, you'll see that the signals your body sends you are relatively clear. To help you stop eating at the end of the meal and snacking after meals, just clean your teeth and move onto another activity. The taste of toothpaste will definitely stop you wanting to eat again if you have any love for food.

Watch out for fake hunger

We can feel a desire to eat for different reasons: stress or anxiety, a lack of love, the desire for pleasure or after seeing an advert for something that looks really delicious that we would have liked to eat. This is fake hunger – generally these desires pass quickly as long as you're able to detect them and distinguish them from true hunger.

In most cases, the body has absolutely no need to eat. There is another need to satisfy. You need to learn to better understand what's going on in your body to identify the needs it's expressing at these times. By identifying the real need, you'll be able to effectively satisfy it.

For example, if your body is stressed or anxious and needs comforting, the mere fact of remembering a pleasant moment spent with loved ones can provide the necessary comfort. It's not necessary to eat a chunk of chocolate. Just thinking can be enough.

I remember a patient who, every evening, would eat cakes from his home country, which he had left many years before. Eating these cakes allowed him to reconnect with his happy childhood memories, and at these times, this sixty year old man became a small boy again. He felt all the pleasure of being a small boy in the country of his childhood, with the people around him who loved him at that time. He didn't eat because he was hungry, but because of nostalgia.

I suggested a simple exercise: to spend some time in the evening remembering his childhood, looking at old photos, reading stories about his country...in short I suggested a way other than food of entering that state his body felt it needed. By doing these exercises, he totally overcame his addiction. From time to time he would eat those delicious cakes because he liked them, but in much more reasonable quantities.

To another patient, who needed to relax after a long, hard day at work, I suggested getting a foot massage. Rather than eating, she could relax and feel good simply by getting a massage. In Thailand, couples take massages regularly. The pleasure a massage gives is extraordinary, and is a perfect substitute for the pleasure you get by eating a packet of biscuits for example. I say that because many couples don't know how to enjoy themselves.

Food is an easy and cheap pleasure, but it's not the only one. You just need to learn what they are. If food is a source of pleasure in your life, you can't just get rid of it without replacing it with something else. That wouldn't work. So you need to find something enjoyable to replace eating, find another activity which completely satisfies your need at that time. Because once again, your body doesn't need to eat. It needs gentleness, tenderness and affection in most cases.

LIVE IN THE NOW
TO FEEL BETTER

Earlier we discussed the case of people suffering from stress and anxiety. Often people suffering from stress and anxiety don't live in the present. They are totally disconnected, fixated on their plans or personal or professional concerns. They may be right in front of you but their mind is elsewhere, mulling over some important problem. That's what makes them eat too much when they take a break. Because they're not listening to anything their body tells them. They've stopped listening to their body.

The body has many ways of sending signals to your conscious mind. Pain, tiredness or irritation, are all signals you can hear and understand and should take into account. Stressed people don't listen to any of these signals. With over nutrition and malnutrition, we see the same process. The body tells you: "That's it. I've eaten too much, or I don't want to eat any more of this food because it makes me ill". But the mind doesn't listen.

Just ignore it!

I don't know how many times I've heard this phrase from my parents, who in turn heard it from my grandparents, who in turn learnt it from my great grandparents! This phrase sums up modern western culture. You shouldn't listen to what your body says because if you listen, you'll make nothing of your life. It's as if listening to your body was a mistake. Yet in health matters it's quite the reverse.

Gastric reflux, bloating, stomach cramps, constipation, diarrhoea and piles are all signs of an unbalanced diet that are rarely listened to. Instead, people try and mask the symptoms by taking drugs. People really torment their body. The body is required to suffer every trial, difficulty and pain, and isn't even allowed to complain. The body is seen as a machine or slave which must obey.

This attitude to the body is particularly prevalent when doing physical activities or sport. When you learn to do sport at school or in a club, it always involves suffering. You have to go beyond your limits, learn to excel, and for this you need to suffer through gruelling training. Of course this training causes injuries…but it's not serious, you need to work through the pain! Sport is designed as a way of learning to ignoring pain, instead of being a tool for pleasure, fun and enjoyment.

A great jog

One day a friend of mine, Sylvie, invited me to go jogging with her group. The leader was an old man who had once been a prize-winning marathon runner.

He offered slightly unusual runs through the forest. His goal was to make us run, but with the greatest possible amount of pleasure. Unusual, no?

I must admit that I learnt to do sport through suffering, pitting my mind against my body. I learnt to go beyond my limits, go beyond my suffering and above all not to listen to my body, to go ever further and faster. I ask myself why: I'm not destined to become a top sportsman. I don't think I have the ambition or the skill.

When I went running I would set a goal, timing myself with my watch. At school, we learnt that to run fast and run for a long time, above all we needed to practice regularly. So I put these wise words into practice. Each time, I tried to improve my performance by reaching my limits.

On that day, with this old man, a small group of us ran through the forest. There were people of different ages and different abilities. When we were tired we were allowed to stop. Sometimes he suggested we speed up, taking pleasure in going fast. Speed and feeling the wind on your face and the legs that carry us, is nice.

We had to listen to what we were feeling. The old man said: "listen to what's happening inside you, speed up when you want to and slow down when you want to". I loved speeding up and then walking peacefully, listening to my heartbeat.

I think it was that day I learned to run and jog. I learnt to do sport for fun, and to feel better. I understood why so many people hate sport and refuse to do it. They're just afraid of hurting themselves, and I understand that. Because there's no point in hurting yourself.

Doing sport is vital because the body needs exercise and it needs pleasure. Doing sport is a form of care. By doing sport you're looking after yourself, getting rid of stress and tension. You strengthen your back and your heart, weakened by your sedentary life. You clear your mind. You focus on the here and now.

Sport is an amazing activity which lets you feel completely in the moment if you do it for that very purpose, feeling good. Feeling good, let that be your new philosophy. Everything you do should be seen as a type of self-care.

Forget what your teachers, parents and educators told you. Everything they taught you about your body is wrong. It's not their fault. They were also taught wrong things about the body. The important thing is to know that you're mistaken, accept it and take the true path.

BE MINDFUL WHILE YOU EAT

When you eat, you're often thinking about something else. How many people eat in front of the TV, thinking about their plans, their concerns, their goals? They are disconnected from what they eat, and they're not thinking about what they're eating, they tend to eat too much and poorly. This disconnect is common among the overweight, who fail to pay attention to what they're eating. When stressed, they're capable of eating a bag of crisps in front of the TV without even noticing.

If you want to lose weight you need to relearn how to eat. Relearning how to eat means learning how to eat mindfully. Eating mindfully means eating while being in the here and now, connected to your body. Being connected to your body means fully feeling the sensations your body gives off when you eat. This means the sensations that come from all the organs involved in the whole food and digestion cycle.

- The eyes that perceive the colour and shape of foods,
- The nose which perceives the aromas the dish gives off,
- The lips, the tongue, the palate, the inside of your cheeks which perceive flavours,
- The gums and teeth which cut, crush, mix,
- The salivary glands that produce saliva to facilitate digestion,
- The throat which contracts so you can swallow,

- The muscles of the oesophagus which contract to push food down,
- The stomach which fills with gastric juices and dissolves food,
- The intestines that break food down into nutrients,
- How long is it since you took the time to really look at what you eat, took the time to really smell its aroma before putting it in your mouth?
- How long is it since you really chewed each piece of food, swallowed and felt the sensation it produces when it enters your stomach?
- Eating mindfully means paying attention to all these sensations. This means that your attention must be focused on the here and now.
- It means paying attention when you eat, as if performing a highly complex task which the slightest lapse could mess up.
- The next time you eat, take the time:
- To look with your eyes,
- To smell with your nose,
- To detect all the flavours with your tongue,
- To chew until the food becomes liquid,
- To feel the food going down your throat,
- To feel the food entering your stomach,

We often forget how important eating is. The profusion of foods in modern society has made it a commonplace activity yet if you think about it, this profusion is extremely recent, going back a century at most. So we need to be aware of how lucky we are to be able to eat when we're hungry. Eating is an important event in your day, a sacred moment because it's the moment you give your body the elements it needs to survive.

You will agree with me when I say that life is the most precious thing any human being owns. That's why eating is such an important moment. It's when you preserve life, care for life, nurture the life within you. That's why you need to spend time carefully choosing the food you eat, deciding how to cook it and spending time eating it. Eating is like caring for yourself, and this is something that can't be rushed.

LEARN HOW TO DO NOTHING

I think that was the hardest thing I had to deal with when losing weight: learning how to do nothing. We spend our time trying to fill time. As soon as we have a free second, we use it, we do something: read, play, watch TV, work, look after the kids, go to the cinema or theatre, do the gardening or DIY etc. We're constantly trying to fill our lives with as many activities as possible. In this way we feel replete.

Personally, I'm always very busy. My role as CEO and therapist keep me really busy all day long, and it's in the evenings when I suddenly have nothing to do. I find myself at home, suddenly all alone without anything in particular to do. That's when I get a feeling of emptiness, and this makes me anxious. Suddenly, the very fact of stopping everything made me face up to a stressful life. For years I used to fill that emptiness by eating.

Eating lets you feel things: feelings in your mouth and also your stomach. By eating you receive stimuli. I think that eating fills the gap created by the lack of stimulation. Emptiness could be described as feeling nothing in particular. You're at an in-between state where you experience and feel nothing in particular. Your general state is neutral. I think that moment is particularly critical because the absence of stimulation creates anxiety. It's as if we aren't really living any more.

I think that if you want to stop eating too much, especially in the evenings, you need to learn to manage this feeling of emptiness. You need to learn to be alive without necessarily having any stimuli or sensations. You need to learn how to be in a neutral state. You need to learn to live less intensely. You need to learn to live by just being. Basically, you need to learn to do nothing, just to do nothing and feel good in that state. For highly active people, this is really complicated.

I remember a Quebecois therapist I went to one day. He offered hypnotherapy sessions with the aim of learning to "do nothing". I've rarely felt as much pleasure as during this session, which just involved closing your eyes and doing nothing. Giving myself permission to do nothing was incredibly relaxing, calming. Doing nothing means acceptance of just being, without a purpose or function other than just being there. You're doing nothing, you're learning nothing, you're not developing. Nothing is happening.

Boredom has always scared me. But I think I need to face up to it. Because if I don't face up to boredom, I'll never be able to stop eating in the evenings. That's my final challenge, the thing that will free me from all the rest, and allow me to live to a healthy old age. Accepting boredom, doing nothing, just means facing up to the passage of time, facing up to yourself and accepting the feelings that come from your body at that time, it means accepting emptiness. Accepting emptiness means freeing yourself from the need to fill it, and therefore the need to eat to feel replete.

EXPERT SCIENTIFIC OPINION ON THE LINK BETWEEN BODY AND MIND: "THE SECOND BRAIN"

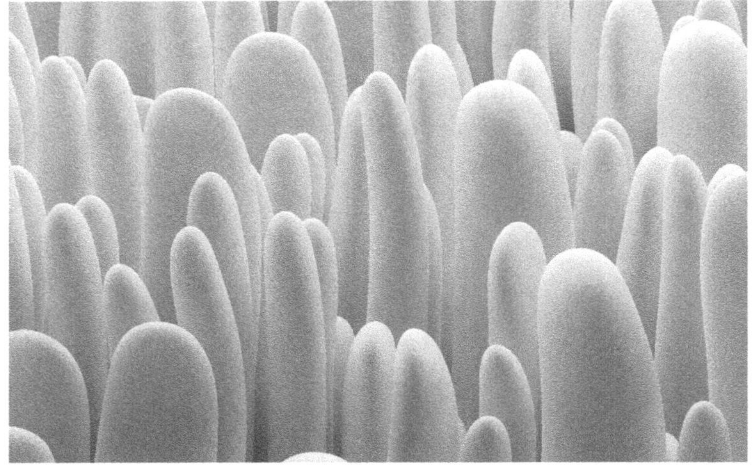

Scientists have recently discovered that our stomach contains almost two hundred million neurons, as many as the brain of a cat or dog. Our stomach hides a true miracle of intelligence that manages our digestion: our "second brain". This second brain is independent, and its scientific name is the enteric nervous system. Researchers have discovered that this "second brain" communicates with our higher brain, that there are conversations between the two.

① THE STOMACH COMMUNICATES WITH THE BRAIN

The enteric nervous system is above all responsible for managing the contraction of muscles necessary for digestion. It also ensures the mixing of foods in the stomach and regulates the bio-chemical environment, particularly digestive enzymes and gastric juices. It also protects the body against bacteria and viruses. If an intruder enters the body, the enteric nervous system will provoke vomiting or diarrhoea to get rid of it. It therefore has a vital role in the survival of the body.

But the most surprising thing is the discovery by scientists in the 90s of the role of the enteric brain in the regulation of emotions. Neurons in the enteric nervous system secret as much dopamine as the higher brain! Dopamine is the hormone of happiness and reward. It is responsible for the feeling of fullness after meals. It is also responsible for the feeling of joy after giving or receiving a kiss. Even more surprising, this second brain secretes 95% of the body's serotonin!

And serotonin is essential for mental balance. A lack of serotonin will cause stress and anxiety which can result in behavioural issues like phobias. Serotonin also controls body temperature and circadian rhythms which regulate sleep. Finally, the serotonin secreted by the enteric nervous system stimulates the repair of cells damaged in the lungs and liver. It also helps the heart to function and regulates bone density. The enteric nervous system is therefore essential for good health.

② WHEN INTESTINAL BACTERIA COMMUNICATE WITH THE BRAIN

Latest research has come up with some even more surprising results. While it has now been proven that the "stomach communicates with the brain", new discoveries have shown that the enteric nervous system communicates with bacteria present in the intestines, what we call microbiota. A Canadian research team conducted different experiments on mice as part of the international MetaHit project (METAgenomics of the Human Intestinal Tract). These were the results.

Experiments were conducted on mice. Firstly, researchers gave antibiotics to mice for 7 days. And they found that antibiotic treatment disrupted intestinal flora, and that this disruption caused the mice anxiety. Put another way, they showed that if intestinal flora was disrupted, it influenced the mice's mood. So food can have an impact on stress, anxiety and depression, because we know that it influences the microbiota.

In a second experiment, scientists bred two types of rats. Their temperament varied according to the bacteria contained in their microbiota. The first batch of mice was introverted and anxious, while the others were much bolder, extravert and curious. In parallel, mice lacking intestinal bacteria, because they were bred in a sterile environment, had microbiota from the two batches transplanted into them. And the results obtained were undeniable: the animals "inherited" the characteristics of the "donor" mice:

In a third experiment, the same Canadian team demonstrated that while intestinal flora could influence mood or character, mood and character could in turn influence intestinal flora. Scientists performed an ablation of the mice's olfactory bulbs, which had the effect of making the animals anxious and highly sensitive to stress. After the operation, they recorded disruption of the intestinal flora, as well as an increase in the brain of CRF rates, a stress neurotransmitter released by the hypothalamus.

All this research shows how much the body and mind are linked. They show that the way we view illness and food is far removed from reality. We should consider the human being not as an isolated being but more like an ecosystem. This ecosystem influences its health and well-being. In health and wellbeing, food plays a central role because it can stress the nervous system located in the intestines. It is almost certain that eating too much and poorly will have an impact on the enteric nervous system which will be stressed. This will also have repercussions on intestinal flora. And this in turn will lead to psychological problems (stress, anxiety, malaise, dark thoughts). I am what I eat. Over 2,000 y ears ago, Hippocrates said: "Let food be thy medicine!" And he wasn't wrong. In any event, this is what recent scientific studies have shown.

EXERCISE:
EATING MINDFULLY

A note on visualisation techniques

Visualisation techniques are powerful techniques used in psychology and coaching to reprogram your thinking and behaviour. The more seriously you take the visualisation techniques suggested in this book, the quicker you'll get results. Whenever you do the exercises, make sure you concentrate and visualise things as precisely as possible. At first, you might find it a bit difficult, but by persevering the images will appear and you'll see the effects. To develop your capacity to visualise, do the following exercise before doing the exercise suggested in the book:

- *Visualise a colour in your mind. Think of a colour that evokes pleasant memories/ sensations for you.*
- *Then think of a sound. It could be a piece of music or just a simple sound that evokes pleasant memories/ sensations for you.*
- *Then think of a smell. Recall a smell that evokes pleasant memories/ sensations for you.*

- *Then think of a taste, the taste of a good or anything else that evokes pleasant sensations/memories for you.*
- *Finally, think of a physical sensation: a caress, the feeling of the wind on your face or any other pleasant sensation.*

Do this exercise with your eyes closed in a peaceful spot. As you'll find out, it helps you slow down and develop your concentration skills.

First, I'd like you to focus on a very special part of your body.

I'd like you to focus on that particular part of your body located between the tip of your nose and the top part of your lips.

I'd like you to feel all the sensations that come from this part and this part alone of your body.

Focus on all the sensations that come from it. Feel the air that caresses it each time you inhale.

Feel the gentle freshness when you inhale, and the gentle sense of warmth when you exhale.

Focus.

• • •

When you are perfectly aware of the sensations coming from this part of the body, and only when you can only feel these sensations, I'd like you to shift your attention to the edge of your lips, as if you were stroking them delicately with your fingers.

Move your focus around your lips. On the top of your lips.

The focus on the inside of your lips. Feel their thickness, their warmth, their sensitivity.

Then shift your focus to the corners of your lips. Feel the unique sensations coming from this particular place.

Then move inside your mouth.

• • •

Feel your teeth, how they're aligned in your mouth, held by your gums. Make the inside of your mouth your palace, the inside of your cheeks your language.

Focus on the tip of your tongue and activate the millions of taste buds covering its surface.

Firstly the taste buds on the tip of the tongue. Then those on the side. Then those on the back of the tongue.

Each part is responsible for perceiving taste.

• • •

Then go down your throat. Feel the sensations of your tonsils and then your pharynx.

Then move down to your oesophagus. Then move down to your stomach.

Feel the walls of your stomach. Feel its shape, its volume, how it works. How does it feel – good or bad? Is it hungry or resting?

. . .

Now get some food. Whatever you like.

First I'd like you to smell it by placing it right under the nose.

Take the time to breathe in its aroma. Let its aroma enter you. Let the aroma bring back memories, sensations, and intuitions.

Then look at it. Look at its colour and shape.

Now you've smelt it and looked at it properly I'd like you to put it in your mouth.

Chew it.

Feel its composition.

Feel its taste, fell how it spreads around your mouth.

Feel its taste infuse you and let its taste open the door to your memories.

Feel the emotions, ideas and sensations that come to mind when you eat this food.

This food is not merely a taste, a texture, a quantity.

It's also memory, sensations, intuitions. It's also ideas. And when you eat, you're eating all of those things.

Chew it until it becomes liquid in your mouth. Then swallow.

. . .

Feel it pass into your throat, down your oesophagus. Pay attention to everything that's happening within you at that precise moment. Feel it enter your stomach. Listen to what your stomach is telling you at that moment.

Feel it in your stomach, and feel how your whole body reacts to its presence. You should be able to perceive all the mechanisms at work in you at the precise moment the food enters your stomach.

Now feel how this food will be digested by your body. How it will be dissolved before your body ingests it. How these molecules will feed the millions of cells that make up your body.

READ THIS CHILDREN'S STORY: THE INCREDIBLE STORY OF MRS TONGUE

Once there was a great kingdom called the Body. This kingdom extended from the head to the feet, and from the left little finger to the right little finger. It had two long arms and two long legs, a chest, a back and a stomach The Body was a magnificent kingdom full of life, where all the organs lived in peace and happiness. It was ruled by a prince called the Brain. The Brain lived in the head, right at the top of the body, where he could see everything through the eyes, hear everything through the ears and feel everything through the nose.

The Brain played a very important role in the Body. His role was to protect it from harm. For example, he had to make sure the Body didn't trip down stairs, that it didn't get stung by a bee or cut itself with scissors. He also had to eat well to ensure the Body worked properly and didn't get sick. The Brain's role was to help the Body stay healthy and live for as long as possible. To do so, he had to listen to all the other organs, which advised him.

That's why before each meal he would receive each organ (muscle, stomach, intestines, ankles, knees, liver, pancreas, heart, lungs etc.) in his palace to hear their needs. The organs would help him choose what to eat. The legs said: I need milk to grow. The skin said: I need oil to protect myself. The intestines said: I need vegetables to improve my functions. The Brain listened. And then he would order the hands to pick up, and the mouth to chew. And so the Body remained healthy.

But sadly, one of the organs was plotting in secret. She didn't want the Brain and the other organs to decide what she wanted to eat. She wanted to be the Brain instead. This organ was the Tongue. And the Tongue said to herself: I don't see why I should listen to those idiots. They make us eat anything! Yuck. I hate vegetables! As she was the only one able to experience tastes and flavours, she thought she should be the only one to decide what should be eaten. One day she decided to take power.

The Tongue went to see the Brain at the moment he was hungriest. The Brain mainly eats sugars and fats, which are essential for it to function properly. It needs them to think and concentrate and keep quiet in class when the teacher's teaching. It needs them to learn the rules of calculus and multiplication and memorise poems. The Brain needs sugar and fat like a man in the desert needs water. The Tongue had dolled herself up, and most importantly brought a present.

- Hello Brain!
- Hello Tongue, what can I do for you? He asked. But hurry up because I need to do my homework and get something to eat.
- Nothing special, she said, I just wanted to give you a present. It's something I'm sure you'll like.

The Brain, who loved surprises, couldn't wait to see what it was. So the Tongue took a huge lump of white sugar from behind her back. The Brain took a bite. Hmmm…. Right away he felt an incredible sensation, something he'd rarely felt before. He felt stronger, faster, more intelligent. He was like a super brain. Sadly the sensation only lasted a few moments. It disappeared as quickly as it had appeared.

- I don't suppose you've got another present like that, he asked the Tongue. It was really delicious!
- Of course, said the Tongue, who had predicted his reaction. She took another lump of white sugar from behind her back.

The Brain shivered with pleasure. It was so delicious. He felt great! Sadly, like the first time, the pleasure didn't last. On a come down, he asked the Tongue for more sugar. The Tongue have him some more. And this little game continued until the Brain was hooked on sugar. Now the Tongue had the Brain in its power. She could ask him to do anything she wanted. The Brain would obey. The Brain was only thinking of getting more sugar. It's like he was hypnotised.

While the Brain was busy eating sugar, the Tongue took the opportunity to seize his crown. She proclaimed herself Queen of the Body. Now she was the boss! As soon as she became Queen, she ordered the hands to pick up any cakes, sweets or ice creams they came across. The eyes were ordered to seek out sugar and fat. And the mouth had to eat them, and the stomach, liver and intestines digest them. She needed sugar and fat to keep the Brain in her power. It was like a spell.

As the Body was only eating ice creams, sweets, cakes, fries and chips, problems soon arose. Several organs became unhappy. The first to complain was the Stomach, who complained of being given too much fatty food in the evening just before going to bed. And he had to work long into the night to digest foods which hadn't even been properly chewed, because Mrs Tongue, craving tastes and flavours, put them into the mouth so quickly. He was really tired.

The Stomach tried to complain to the Brain by sending him messages. He triggered horrible pains in the stomach. But the Brain wasn't listening. He would only listen to the Tongue and her pretty words. The intestines, deprived of vegetables and required to digest large quantities of pasta and pizza, could no longer defecate. A huge blockage formed. The Body could no longer go to the toilet. The Throat also complained at the ice creams which chilled it and gave it sore throats. In the Body, the organs were suffering.

The Tongue drowned out all the complaints of the other organs with her wheezy voice: ignore them Brain, they're bad organs. They're just jealous. It's up to you to decide what you eat. You're the boss! And the Brain listened. He even became annoyed at the other organs who had used to be his friends. Instead of listening to them, the Brain went to the doctor, who prescribed him different drugs. And with these treatments the organs lost their ability to complain. They had to suffer in silence.

As it ate, the Body got fat and the number of unhappy organs increased. The stomach and the thighs could no longer store all that fat. The knees and the ankles were suffering from carrying all that weight. The back was tired of keeping the body upright and cried every day. Not to mention the fact that, obsessed with fatty and sugary food, the Brain had stopped ordering the muscles to function. The muscles had melted. The lungs were faltering. The heart was palpitating. The Body lost its ability to do sport.

And then, one day, things started getting really bad. The stomach had burnt the oesophagus with its gastric juices. The lungs, inflamed by juices, suffered from asthma and started to wheeze. The intestines were on fire and, without rhyme or reason, would become constipated or cause diarrhoea. The liver and the pancreas were ill from all that sugar, and at risk of diabetes. Even the Tongue started to feel bad. The Tongue was really in a bad way. It had become ill from food. It's like it had been poisoned.

The Brain realised that something wasn't right. He also felt really bad. So he went to the doctor. For the first time in his life he told the Brain off. He was eating way too much, and all the wrong things! Things had to change or he risked endangering the Body. The Body could die! This was a wakeup call for the Brain. And then he remembered the promise he had once made to care for the Body and help it live to a healthy old age. Suddenly he took a big decision. He decided to change.

The first thing he did was pay a visit to each organ, to listen to them. He visited the Stomach, the Intestines, the Liver, the Pancreas, the kidneys, the Knees, the Ankles, the Back, even the Bile duct and the Spleen. Everyone had the right to an audience. The Brain listened carefully to everyone. He realised how much all the organs were suffering. He heard their suffering and realised he'd been wrong. He'd only been thinking of himself. He'd been acting selfishly without thinking of the consequences.

Of course the Tongue, seeing that he was about to escape her clutches, tried to charm him again. She filled his mind with memories of the delicious taste of vanilla ice cream and chocolate cakes. She reminded him of the pleasure he felt when devouring a bag of sweets in front of a cartoon on the TV, when he ate fries in the canteen and crisps for snacks. But the Brain wasn't listening any more. He'd made his decision. He'd realised that he hadn't been eating food but poison.

The next day the Brain did a huge spring clean of the house the Body lived in. He threw out all the foods that contained too much sugar and fat. He joined a gym and bought a bike so he could do sport every day. He decided to watch less TV and go on long walks instead. And later that day, when he went to do his groceries at the supermarket, he made sure he consulted all the organs before deciding what he should cook and eat. He wanted to be healthy!

Before putting food in his basket, he would ask: the Tongue says it's good but what do you think? The Stomach, the Intestines, the Liver, the Pancreas, the kidneys, the Knees, the Ankles, the Back, even the Bile duct and the Spleen, would answer him. He realised that certain foods the Tongue loved didn't go down at all well with the other organs, although some were liked by both. The other organs had the final decision. And when he ate, he would ask them how much to eat.

From that day he realised that if you want a healthy Body, you need to listen to what each part of it wants. He ensured that every part of the body maintained good relations with each other, respecting them and caring for them, like a conductor who cares for each of his musicians and helps them to produce a harmonious melody. And in this way he took on the task of caring for his most precious asset.

The Body understood that there were many other pleasures in life than the Tongue had been offering: doing sport, reading, playing, talking, dreaming, walking etc. There are so many things to do, so many passions to feel, so many shows to watch, that life wouldn't suffer. The simple act of breathing and feeling your heart beat should be a source of immense satisfaction in itself. The very feeling of being alive is a source of infinite pleasure. There are more things than the Tongue in life – there are also the ears, the eyes, the skin and the nose... There are many other things to eat. There are many other foods.

6 THINGS TO AVOID WHILE EATING TO LOSE WEIGHT AND LIVE LONGER

---

1 EATING WHILE WATCHING TV

The television captures our attention and stops us focusing on ourselves and its real needs. Turn your TV off if you really want to eat mindfully. And above all, don't eat while watching the news, which causes anxiety and so disrupts the emotional centres found in the "second brain" which is our digestive system.

2 EATING WHILE READING A BOOK

Reading the newspaper while eating is just putting bad news on your plate. Reading a good novel is an opportunity to travel and dream, but makes us forget what we're eating. If we forget what we're eating we will miss the signals from our body telling us that we're hungry or full.

3 EATING WHILE SURFING THE INTERNET

In restaurants these days you see tons of people with their eyes fixated on their smartphone screen. They're there but not really there. They aren't really making the most of their meals. Eating is more than feeling the taste of a food; it's also looking at it, feeling it with your nostrils. It's being in the here and now.

4 EATING WHILE WORRYING

There's no need to think about your problems to find a solution. Don't worry, your brain will continue to work and find solutions even if you're not thinking of them. If you're focused on your problems when you eat, you'll end up disrupting your nervous system because of all the negative emotions you're experiencing.

5 EATING WHILE ARGUING

The same thing happens when you eat while arguing. Anger, sadness, aggression, all these emotions disrupt the digestive system. Make the kitchen a sacred place where arguments are banned, because this is the surest way of causing stomach ache. If this doesn't work, then it's better to eat alone.

6 EATING WHILE DRIVING

Some people are in such a hurry that they don't even take the time to stop and eat. For one thing it's dangerous, because you risk having an accident. What a shame to risk your life and that of others just to save a few minutes! Not to mention the fact that you run the risk of eating extremely badly.

Eating is a time of pleasure and relaxation. It's the perfect time to be in the here and now, paying attention to what's happening in your body. By focusing on what you're doing and what you feel, you'll be able to loosen up and take a real break from the day, especially if work is getting you down.

Taking time at breakfast, lunch and dinner is really vital.

Personally, on my path to a new lifestyle, on which this book is a milestone, I still haven't reached this goal. Sometimes I don't even have five minutes for lunch because I've agreed to too many meetings. I do this to make sure I'm available to my many patients.

I realise what a mistake this is, because it tires me out. I'm then less effective, and above all my health suffers. Helping others and being useful is important but not at the cost of your health. It's better to live a long life and help people over the long term than trying to do everything at once.

Life is a marathon, not a sprint. We always want things to move faster. We demand immediate satisfaction. We need to learn to wait. By caring for ourselves, our body and mind, we give ourselves the chance to see our wildest dreams become a reality one day.

STAGE 5:
TAKE UP A PHYSICAL ACTIVITY

STAGE 5:
TAKE UP A PHYSICAL ACTIVITY

---

① TO CONSUME MORE ENERGY

To lose weight you really only have two options:

- **Option 1:** consume less energy by reducing the amount of food you eat and/or changing the structure of your food. You eat smaller quantities of lower calorie foods. For example, you decide to eat 500g of grated carrots instead of 1 kg of vanilla ice cream. Your nutritional intake will evidently fall. If you rebalance your diet like this, you'll lose weight. You'll be adopting a new, healthy diet and will never go back, because you know that this is the right food for you.
- **Option 2:** increase the amount of energy you consume by increasing your physical activity. Your muscles consume huge amounts of energy, so if you use them more, and more often, they will consume the energy provided by food. Your body should draw on its reserves. You'll lose weight automatically. But note that when I say lose weight, I mean you'll lose "bad weight", represented by fat. You will replace fat with muscle. What counts is not so much losing weight as rebalancing your body mass by increasing muscle mass to the detriment of fatty mass.

The program I'm suggesting aims to balance the two options. On the one hand you should eat fewer toxic fatty or sugary foods, while increasing your consumption of low calorie foods like fruit and vegetables. On the other, you need to increase your daily physical activity to increase the energy you consume. In this way you'll boost your dynamism and appetite for action. The more you move about, the more you'll feel like moving, and the more energy you'll consume.

Once you've adopted these new healthy living habits, you need to make sure you keep them up. The aim isn't just to eat better and do more sport for a month to lose weight, for example just after winter (a lot of people do that). The aim is to eat better and do sport for the rest of your life, so you develop habits that protect and care for your body. In this weight you'll lose weight and live longer.

You'll learn to eat differently. You'll take great pleasure in it, because eating differently will get you in tune with your body. Your body will become a constant source of satisfaction and well-being. You'll learn to do sport and enjoy it, because it gives you energy. It will give so much pleasure, wellbeing and satisfaction that soon you'll be hooked. I know people over 80 who're still working and doing sport!

And I'll repeat it, because it's essential: this book isn't suggesting a diet. The idea isn't to deprive yourself of food for 1 month while swimming for 3 hours a day. If you do this, as soon as you stop you'll regain all the weight lost in the blink of an eye. You even risk putting more back on than you had lost. Diets are like boomerangs. If you don't pay attention you'll end up getting fat again, because the body has an extraordinary ability to fight deprivation.

The aim of this book is to progressively and sustainable change your diet and habits while developing a real pleasure in eating healthy foods, while making regular physical activity a source of pleasure, relaxation and satisfaction.

It's a life in which you listen to yourself, your body and its real needs: a complete philosophy for living. This isn't the way most people live. This program invites you to live differently.

- Are you ready to live differently to others?
- Are you ready to commit to caring for your body?
- Are you ready to stop living with stress and anxiety?
- Are you ready to love yourself and do all you can to be healthy and feel good?
- Are you ready to stop listening to the marketing men?
- Are you ready to reinvent your life?

If you've answered "YES" to all these questions, then keep reading – you're ready to commit to this program. If you've answered "NO" to any question, then stop reading and carry on like before. In the end, nobody's forcing you to be healthy, be in shape and live a long life. You have the right, you are free, to eat all the fatty and sugary foods you want, if you feel like it. I'm merely suggesting you decide to follow another path. It's up to you.

As I mentioned above, by taking up a physical activity, you will replace fat with muscle. Some patients who follow our programs might complain of not losing weight quickly enough. They'd like to lose 5-6 kilos (11-13 lbs.) in a week. The problem is that in almost all diets, this weight loss is at the cost of the muscles. They think they've lost their excess weight, but this weight has come from their muscles.

The loss of muscle mass causes the metabolism to slow down. Put another way, as you have less muscle and muscles are big consumers of calories, your body consumes fewer calories. As it consumes fewer calories, you need to eat less to avoid putting on weight. It's a vicious circle: the more weight you lose, the more you have to deprive yourself to avoid putting on weight. This is why we talk about the "yoyo diet". You always put on the weight lost after a strict diet.

The best strategy is to put on the muscle lost when losing weight at the start of the program. For this you need to take up a physical activity, and above all maintain a balanced diet. By strengthening your muscles you speed up your metabolism, and therefore its consumption of calories, so you lose weight more quickly, particularly fat. It's s virtuous circle. What's great is that people who don't do any physical activity can thus expect faster loss of weight in fat.

The other benefit of developing muscles while losing fat is that muscles take up less room. The body becomes trimmer, more contoured. So you might not weigh less on the scales but drop a clothes size. When you don't have the equipment necessary to measure your fat and muscle rates, you need to rely on your clothes. If they start feeling looser, you're on the right path! Once again, the aim of this program is for you to listen more to your body, without relying on external indicators.

The virtuous circle of physical activity

I started doing sport again a few months ago. While performing visualisation exercises with my patients, I ended up influencing myself.

This is the paradox of therapists – they end up treating themselves while treating their patients!

So I got an exercise bike. At first I used it every two or three days for about 15 minutes. Gradually I felt like I wanted to do more, and moved on to 30 minutes almost every day. Before, I would come up with excuses. I'd tell myself: "I really don't have the time. I have much more important things to do". Then suddenly my approach changed; what became important to me was getting on the bike and pedalling. I experienced a real feeling of relaxation and well-being, especially after taking a nice hot shower right afterwards.

At first, getting on the bike required discipline and will. To be honest, I had to force myself because I would get really bored on the bike and pedalling was tiring... But of course it was – my muscles hadn't worked for months!

But gradually, obligation turned into a need. That's how the brain works: when it gets used to doing something it gets hooked. It's hard at first and then it's impossible to do without it.

I needed to get on my bike or I would feel bad. So I got on the bike every day after work, generally late in the evening. It made me felt great, relaxing and calming me.

To avoid getting bored I went on YouTube and watched conferences on interesting subjects, I read, I worked on my English or played chess while pedalling. Learning or playing while pedalling is a good way of avoiding boredom.

Then I started fancying other sports. I bought other equipment. I dusted off the dumbbells I had used when I was 18 and started body building.

More and more, my body wanted to do exercise. It felt so good that it wanted to prolong the pleasure. Strange! Just a few weeks before, it was pure suffering and something I had to force myself to do, and now it was a time of enjoyment.

I also set up a punch bag, because I love boxing, and started using a skipping rope ("Heath rope!"). Six months after I had finally got an exercise bike, under the influence of visualisation, I was doing over an hour of sport each day.

I felt ten years younger. I wanted to do more and more exercise. I started walking or cycling instead of driving. When I listened to music, I felt like dancing, and did so. My body was following the rhythm of its own volition!

I noticed I had a lot more energy in my day to day activities. I wanted to move about more, spend my free time outside. Before, on my days off I used to be very tired and stay at home to relax by reading or watching films.

Now I wanted to take walks in the forest, go to dance classes, learn how to sing... I wanted to get out, be active. Of course, when you start going out more, and when you're active, you spend less time eating.

Going out really relaxed me and stopped me fixating on my professional or personal plans, which really helped me reduce my stress. It also made me more creative.

I was really surprised to see this transformation in just a few months. What most surprised me was how much younger I felt. I'm thirty six but I felt twenty five!

When I used to be overweight I felt like I was 50! I was wrong. It was all down to my lifestyle!

In my circle I know 70 year olds who still go jogging, go out with friends every evening and run a company. François Roustang, the man who taught me hypnosis, is still, at almost 95, giving classes to over 100 people at the weekends. He has a vivacity of mind and body that many young people would envy. I also know people over sixty who spend all their time sat in front of the TV. They think they're too old to be active. They're old and behave like old people simply because they think they're old. But they're wrong. An extraordinary life which just needs awakening lies dormant within them.

The differences observed in the effect of age on the body and mind are not linked to genetics, they're above all linked to state of mind! By eating healthily, by losing weight, by taking up a physical activity, these persons can feel younger and regain the skills they thought they'd lost for good (and even discover new ones!). The worst thing is that these people don't realise that their sedentary lifestyle will make them old before their time. It's this, and not their age, which will soon make them disabled. I can say this because I'm young and I've experienced it

When I was twenty-nine, I went to visit my wife's family. Her father and grandparents on both sides live in the Russian speaking part of the Ukraine (near the Crimea, currently at war). At that time I was suffering from pains in my back and spine, and was finding it hard to turn my head... I was constantly aching all over. And I couldn't stand up for more than an hour without feeling the need to sit or lie down. My wife's grandfather, a former miner, was then 72. And he would do exercises on the high bar... He would throw his legs in the air while spinning round the bar and laughing like a child! I couldn't believe my eyes.

What was his secret?

- *Firstly, every day he would eat fruits and vegetables grown with love in his own garden. The fruits and vegetables they grow in that country are the best I've ever eaten, because of the soil, which is the best in the world, but also because the varieties they grow there are very ancient. Unlike in industrialised countries they haven't been selected for their size or been genetically modified. Obviously all these fruits and vegetables are organic.*
- *Then he did sport every day. He travelled to his garden by bike and spent the morning working on his vegetable patch. And then he'd come back home and take a siesta. After that he'd go back to his vegetable patch. Every day he'd do press-ups and stretches and practice on the high bar. In our country, people are in such a hurry*

to retire…but being in a hurry to retire is like being in a hurry to die! Indeed, work stimulates your mind and body (as long as your job isn't too sedentary).

I have only one piece of advice to give you. If you want to live to a healthy old age, never stop working. Continue to do physical and mental exercise no matter how old you are. You don't necessarily have to work for a company or an administration. You could join an association. You could create your own company. No matter how you do it, the main thing is to be active and useful. You need to continue working your body and mind. This is the best way of staying healthy.

Whatever your age, remember it's never too late to change your life!

EXTEND YOUR LIFE SPAN

A sedentary life is one of causes of illness we mention nowhere near enough. Yet all scientific studies show that a sedentary life significantly increases:

- The risk of cardio-vascular illnesses,
- The risk of osteoporosis,
- The risk of certain cancers,
- The risk of diabetes,
- The risk of obesity

The more active you are, the healthier you'll be!

The vicious circle of a sedentary life and the virtuous circle of movement

The less active you are, the more your muscles atrophy, the more your metabolism slows, the greater your risk of putting on weight. The more weight you put on, the less active you'll feel like being, the more your muscles atrophy, the harder it is to move about etc. The more sedentary you are, the greater your chances of suffering conditions linked to a sedentary life. These pains cause stress that you might try and reduce by consuming more food. Sources of pleasure also reduce, leading to over eating, simply because when we're more sedentary, we have access to fewer sources of pleasure and satisfaction!

The more active you are, the more your muscles develop, the more your metabolism increases, the more chance you have of losing weight and the fewer muscle or joint pains you will have. You're mobile, agile, flexible. You consume energy and therefore lose weight. You're in rude health and you want to stay that way. It's an act of day to day maintenance. You feel more comfortable in your head and body. You're more open to going out and doing things outside, finding pleasure at meeting people and discovering new things and experiences. You're well-nourished and don't feel like snacking any more!

I know of what I speak because I have personal experience of the effects of being overweight. When I was 30 kg (66 lbs.) overweight, I had a really bad back. After a day at work, I was exhausted. I often had a bad neck because of being seated all day. When I travelled I found it really hard to stand up for long. I've always loved travelling, walking, visiting exhibitions and museums. But because I was overweight, I was always tired. It's like I found it hard to carry myself.

It prevented me from doing a lot of things I would have liked to do. It was limiting my possibilities. It was reducing my freedom. When I climbed stairs or walked too quickly, I was out of breath. I was 1.95 m (6.4 foot), and felt like a huge ship, slow and difficult to manoeuvre. The worst was when I went to Paris and had to take public transport like the metro. Because of my height and excess weight, these trips were exhausting trials.

I was really depressed! How can you feel good in your head when you ache all over? It wasn't possible. I was just thirty and felt like an old man. I admit, I was starting to question my existence. I asked myself: is this what life's about? In the evenings, for comfort and to forget my tiredness and pain, I would prepare huge meals. This soothed me and made me forget the pains of the day. I was really in a bad way. I was very negative.

And then I lost that weight. I did it because I had been forced to. One winter, after eating too much, I had a GERD (gastroesophageal reflux disease). This GERD triggered an asthma attack which turned into chronic bronchitis. Despite the drugs, my health and got worse. In hindsight, I would have never imagined that the mere fact of eating too much could lead to such extremes. Now I understand that eating too much food, especially processed food, is truly poisoning the body.
Because of my health problems I had to profoundly change the way I lived and ate. I tried different diets. I quit lactose, gluten, eggs etc. Until I realised that it was possible to lose weight and restore health and wellbeing by adopting a relatively simple approach to life:

- **Don't eat processed food,**
- **Listen to your body and eat only when you're really hungry,**
- **And do regular physical activity.**

With this new dietary balance and physical activity, my body started to transform. I lost loads of weight. I was more and more honed, increasingly lighter, and more and more energetic and mobile. I had an extraordinary amount of energy. I think I started rejuvenating. I had become younger and had more energy than I had had in at least 10 years. It was incredible. I was eating less, and lots of fruit which was rich in delicious vitamins. I love berries like blackberries, blueberries and raspberries, as well as kiwis and strawberries.

I was going from strength to strength. My body was more flexible. I felt agile. I was full of energy. This treatment of fruits, vegetable and sport was like the fountain of youth. I'd stopped falling ill all the time. It's been several years now since I last fell ill. It's like this regime had given me iron-clad health! How great not to worry about catching a cold at the slightest hint of cold weather. What a great quality of life achieved through a simple method!

Now I don't miss all those ice creams, crisps, fries and pizzas or fast foods, even what others might see as tasty little dishes. They don't interest me anymore because I've discovered a new way of finding pleasure and satisfaction, which is having a healthy body. I've stopped drinking alcohol and I don't miss it at all. I'm not bothered about an aperitif or a barbecue. For me all that's just an illusion, because I know what's really important. And I really have a great life. I'm happy.

GIVE YOUR BODY PERMISSION TO FIND ITS TRUE SELF

The body finds its true self in movement

Recently I went to see a dance performance choreographed by Marie-Claude Pietragala. The whole show was performed by a single dancer. He performed for one hour, with a display of every movement the human body is capable of.

It was extraordinary, very beautiful and impressive. Watching that man, like many others I'm sure, I thought I'd never be able to do what he was doing. It just seemed out of reach.

In thinking that, like everyone else in the room, I was wrong. Maybe I'd never achieve such ease and grace. But if I had a good teacher, if I learnt to use my body, if I trained like that dancer for several hours a day, I could come close to that performance.

Because the only thing that differentiated that man from me was the choices we had made: mine to have a sedentary life, and his to spend his life exploring all

The body is made up of 50% muscle. These muscles are designed to move above. Modern man has forgotten his true nature. Man is designed to stand upright, to walk, to run. Remember the last time you had to do physical work: gardening, painting, moving house etc. You worked all day. It was difficult because you weren't used to it. But in the evening you felt really good. You were hungry and ate with a hearty appetite. And then you slept like a log.

Our modern lives are abnormal. We live removed from nature: the plants, the animals, the stars, the sun, the wind. Living in cities has caused us to forget what nature is. But more than the nature of plants, animals and the elements, we have forgotten our own true nature. Our true nature is surely not to spend all day sat in front of our computer, and the evening in front of a TV screen. Our true nature is movement. Walking, running, jumping, discovering and exploring are in our DNA.

Scientific studies have shown the benefits of movement for thinking, creativity, memory and concentration. Curiously, we think better when we're moving. The Greek philosophers knew the power of movement on the mind. To teach their students they would walk. So Aristotle was the founder of the Peripatetic school, which takes its name from the ancient Greek word peripatetikôs meaning "someone who talks while walking". Put another way, movement stimulates the body but also the mind.

By starting to move about again more and more often, all you're doing is fighting against our abnormal modern lives in western countries. By helping the body rediscover its true self, you will help it work better and be more able to fight the ailments caused by a sedentary life. Paradoxically, people, particularly children, who move about all the time, are sometimes classified as hyperactive. Yet we should stimulate movement, support it and encourage it so we can just be ourselves.

8 TIPS FOR A LESS SEDENTARY LIFE

Achieving a less sedentary life is just a case of doing regular physical activity. But as well as that physical activity, you should also move about regularly during the day. The worst thing is to remain seated all day in front of your computer.

1 STAND UP ONCE AN HOUR

If you do a sedentary job, whether you work behind a computer or spend a long time driving, adopt the habit of taking a break once an hour. Stand up and walk a few steps. Stretch! Take the opportunity to drink a glass of water to hydrate yourself. And instead of sending an e-mail, go and visit your colleagues in other departments.

2 TAKE THE STAIRS INSTEAD OF THE LIFT

When you can, take the stairs. Sometimes we avoid this for fear of becoming out of breath, yet climbing the stairs is a short and intense activity which is great for the heart and an excellent way of cutting down on sedentary activities. Avoid escalators and climb the stairs. Take your time. You don't need to run up them!

❸ WALK SHORT JOURNEYS AND LEAVE YOUR CAR IN THE GARAGE

I know people who use their car to go to the bakery located a few hundred metres from their house to avoid walking. Just walk there! It will do you the world of good and give you an appetite. If you don't like walking, take your bike. It's also good for your health.

❹ WALK YOUR DOG AS OFTEN AS POSSIBLE

Getting out and about more is one of the benefits of owning a pet. Often for these animals this is a joyful moment that I recommend you share as often as possible. Try taking longer walks with your four legged friend. Longer and more frequent, these walks will improve your health.

❺ GET OFF THE BUS OR METRO A STOP EARLY

This is a good technique for walking a bit more in the morning. Rather than remaining seated on public transport, often cramped and uncomfortable, get off the bus or metro one or two stops early and walk. When the weather gets better, take your bike or scooter or simply walk!

⑥ ORGANISE "WALKING MEETINGS"

If you need to catch up with an employee or a colleague, you need to organise a meeting, so why not organise a "walking meeting". Walking through the corridors of your company or even in the heart of nature stimulates discussion, creativity and the absorption of new information, while reducing stress!

⑦ EXPRESS YOUR EMOTIONS THROUGH MOVEMENT

You've just achieved something, you're happy, full of joy, so why not express your emotions through movement? Jump for joy, even if it's just a little jump, raise your hands to the sky, do a victory sign, in short just move. Let movement accompany your emotions. This will give you extraordinary energy.

⑧ DANCE

The body reacts naturally to music. A child who listens to music suddenly feels like moving. When you listen to music, move, free your body. Nobody will judge you. And if you're worried about dancing in public, do it in private. When you get home from work, put some music on and let yourself go.

WHAT SCIENCE TELLS US ABOUT THE BENEFITS OF PHYSICAL ACTIVITY

① THE BENEFITS OF PHYSICAL ACTIVITY ON THE BODY

Physical activity has a host of benefits for the body. These are the main effects observed by researchers and doctors.

- **Reducing ankylosis: ankylosis is the partial or total freezing of a joint.** Specifically, ankylosis takes the form of problems with completely performing a movement, such as being unable to completely turn your neck for example. Physical activity can help you reduce ankylosis by developing your flexibility.

- **Reducing osteoporosis: osteoporosis is a modification of the bone structure.** This modification makes the bones more fragile and leads to a greater chance of breaks. Physical activity strengthens your bones. It prevents you injuring yourself pointlessly. Put another way, you don't run the risk of breaking your leg just because of a fall!

- **Burning excess fat and sugar: if you eat a rich meal or drink alcohol, your body will need to get rid of**

toxins. Physical activity aids with the elimination of these toxins. It will help you feel much better after a rich, boozy meal!

- **Replacing fatty mass with muscle: as we saw above, the more muscle you have, and the faster your metabolism is, the more difficult it is to put on weight and the easier it is to lose.** Physical activity therefore plays a central role in the prevention of weight gain and obesity.

- **Reducing "bad" cholesterol rates: physical activity reduces rates of "bad" cholesterol in the blood, and increases "good cholesterol" which protects veins and arteries.** It thus helps delay hardening of the arteries and reduces the risk of heart attacks and strokes.

- **Increasing your heart rate and regulating blood pressure: the heart is a muscle.** If you make it work, your body will be better supplied. You will avoid hypertension and also prevent bouts of low blood pressure which can cause falls among the elderly.

- **Encouraging good respiratory health: physical activity increases ventilation and circulation in the bronchi and the lungs.** It's an excellent way of ensuring good drainage of bronchial and sinus secretions and clearing blocked noses, so common among people who spend much of their time in overly heated, too dry and sometimes smoky environments. Physical activity is recommended for people who suffer from asthma or bronchial diseases.

- **Encouraging natural, deep and curative sleep: sleep is one of the foundations of good health.** Because it's while you sleep that the body recovers. After a long walk, a good jog or a swim, you'll sleep like a baby, meaning you can recharge your batteries in the long term.

- **Stimulating the immune system: physical activity stimulates the production of immune defences.** Put another way, you will get ill less often if you do regular exercise. No more colds or rhino pharyngitis each time the season changes.

② THE BENEFICIAL EFFECTS OF PHYSICAL ACTIVITY ON THE BRAIN

While scientific studies have long shown the beneficial effects of physical activity on the body, other more recent ones show that physical activity has a positive effect on the functioning of the brain!!! It appears that physical activity boosts brain activity, that it can make us better performing and more intelligent, while protecting the brain from ageing. Thus, several studies have shown that physical activity protects us from dementia, senility and neuro-degenerative illnesses like Alzheimer's.

LESS ANXIETY, LESS DEPRESSION AND LESS NEUROSIS

A study conducted by the Amsterdam Free University in 2006 monitored 19,288 people from adolescence to adulthood over eleven years. This study showed that people who did at least 60 minutes of exercise a week were on average les anxious, less depressed and less nervous, more extraverted and sought more intense sensations than sedentary people. Put another way, if you want to be happy, do regular physical exercise.

BETTER MEMORY

In 2003, a team of scientists from the United Kingdom examined the link between physical activity and memory among 1,919 people. Their level of physical activity was assessed at the age of 36, and then their verbal memory was assessed at 43 and 53. The results of this study show that the more regular physical activity the subjects did at the age of 36, the better their memory in middle age! We knew that memory capacity depended on intellectual training, but now we know that it also depends on physical training.

REGENERATION OF THE BRAIN

Finally, certain studies have shown that muscular activity causes the production of growth factors in the brain. In mice, these growth factors are involved in the formation of neuronal circuits, and are an important regulator of synaptic plasticity. It boosts the creation of micro-vessels and the production of new neurons. Doing regular physical activity stimulates your brain and encourages it to develop and regenerate, whatever your age.

REDUCING THE RISK OF CANCER

A recent piece of research by a team of scientists from the American National Cancer Institute looked at statistical data on almost 1.4 million people who were asked to report their level of physical activity. This data was then compared with occurrences of 26 types of cancer, 186,932 cases of cancer having been identified among the subjects of the study over 17 years. The results showed that subjects who did regular physical activity saw their risk of developing cancer reduce significantly.

Doing sport reduces the risk of cancer of the oesophagus by 42%, liver cancer by 27% and lung cancer by 26%. Overall, doing physical activity reduces the risk of cancer by almost 7%. Researchers emphasise the fact that doing sport is often associated with a healthier lifestyle, which would explain these results. In this respect, 51% of Americans and 31% of people living elsewhere in the world have a level of physical activity below the recommended threshold.

Scientific studies attest to the numerous benefits of physical activity. If you want to feel good and live to a ripe old age, you should do a physical activity every day. You'll soon see that thanks to physical activity, your body will become a constant and inexhaustible source of pleasure, wellbeing and satisfaction. You will no longer need to do over indulge (alcohol, tobacco, fatty or sugary foods) because your body will find pleasure in itself. No more need to look outside your body for pleasure you can find inside!

SPORT AND CALORIES

In terms of energy consumption, physical activities are not equal. Some activities consume more energy than others. Of course you should choose a physical activity to suit your abilities – it's better to do some gentle gymnastics every day than going jogging just once a week. In this area, it's frequency and regularity that counts. It's also better to do something for longer than seeking high intensity exercise.

① CYCLING

Cycling eats up **400 calories** an hour and is recommended for people who want to take up a physical activity because it isn't traumatic. Cycling works the cardio-vascular system and the abdominal, leg and gluteal muscles. It's also perfect for getting back in shape.

② JOGGING

Jogging is perfect for slimming and eating a lot of calories. An hour of jogging eats up on average 600 calories. Running works the cardiovascular system. It restores muscle and tones the back. It strengthens abdominal, leg and gluteal muscles. But be careful – if you're overweight it can be traumatic on the body.

③ BOXING

Boxing is one of my favourite sports. It lets you unwind after work and get rid of stress. Many gyms offer different disciplines (boxing, body combat, fit box etc.). Boxing works the arms, the abdominal muscles and the legs. And in one hour you'll burn between 600 and 800 calories.

④ SKIPPING

All little girls do it when they're little. So, ladies, why not rediscover the sensations of your childhood? But many sports also use it. Indeed, skipping improve coordination. It's excellent for the heart. In terms of slimming, it's perfect for shaping the arms and the calves. Calorie loss is between 800 and 850 calories an hour (of course you don't need to last an hour...).

⑤ SWIMMING

One hour's swimming will make you lose 600 calories on average. Swimming, unlike skipping or jogging, is not traumatic on the body, so is ideal for the overweight. It works all the muscles of the body (shoulders, arms, back, abs, buttocks, legs). Swimming is recommended for people of all ages.

⑥ NORDIC WALKING

Nordic walking will eat up around **300 calories** an hour, which is much less than other activities, except…except you can walk for several hours in a row. A good walk can last 3 or 4 hours, even more, boosting oxygen and losing weight gently, while reconnecting with nature.

⑦ DANCING

Obviously this depends on the type of dance. But you can count on 200 to 300 calories an hour. If you like dancing, do it as much as possible because it improves coordination and stimulates all the muscles of the body. And it's also ideal for people who want to make friends or find love.

⑧ AQUA AEROBICS

Like the above two activities, aqua aerobics is low impact. You can lose **300 calories** on average an hour. The benefit of aqua aerobics is that it isn't traumatic for the body, and it has an effect on cellulite thanks to the massaging effect of the water

For those who want to go a bit further:

Here are a few figures to bear in mind when it comes to enjoying yourself. Because while a physical activity can consume calories, its impact has its limits.

A bar of chocolate = 550 calories = 1 hour of jogging

A large chocolate brownie = 1100 calories = 2 hours of jogging

A packet of biscuits = 1200 calories = 2 hours of skipping

Mass produced food is hyper calorific. Sport isn't enough in itself to consume all the energy it gives you, unless you do it for several hours a day.

MAKE LOVE TO LOSE WEIGHT AND LIVE A HEALTHY LIFE

Making love can consume between 200 and 400 calories, which corresponds to between 30 to 60 minutes on an exercise bike. Obviously you're much less likely to get bored by making love! And this is just the sexual act itself. If you add games and foreplay, you'll get even better results. It's a great way of getting your partner involved in getting in shape. Make love to lose weight and live a healthy life

As well as the energy consumed after a session with your legs in the air, sex is good for the health because it releases different hormones which make you feel good. Making love is an excellent anti-depressant and a smart way of fighting stress and anxiety. The advantage of hormones is that they are all excellent appetite regulators. Finally, among the pleasures that life can offer, sex is among the best. So it's easy to substitute it for your usual square of chocolate!

These are the different hormones secreted by your body when you make love.

❶ PHENYLETHYLAMINE: THE LOVE HORMONE

Phenylethylamine is a hormone released when you fall in love. This hormone has euphoric and stimulating effects. It's what makes us see the world through rose tinted glasses and forget all our partner's little faults! Also, phenylethylamine is a powerful stimulant which tends to make us hyperactive. It makes us want to talk, move about and act more than usual. It's the hormone of movement par excellence. Have you considered falling in love to lose weight?

❷ OXYTOCIN: THE ATTACHMENT HORMONE

Oxytocin is notably produced in large quantities at the moment of orgasm, but also during foreplay, during massages and cuddles. Oxytocin is a hormone produced when two humans strike up a close relationship. In this book we've referred to several studies which show its role in regulating appetite. The more you take time to cuddle, the more of this hormone you produce, the less important eating will seem to you.

③ SEROTONIN:
THE CALMING HORMONE

Serotonin is also produced during sex. This hormone helps you remain optimistic and calm. It's the hormone of calm. Put another way, by making love regularly you risk becoming as wise as the Buddha. More seriously, this hormone will help you reduce your stress and anxiety. It's a vital hormone for good psychological balance. And a good psychological balance, as we've seen, is the best way of staying slim.

④ DOPAMINE:
THE REWARD HORMONE

Dopamine is the reward hormone. Rather than eating when you fancy a bar of chocolate or biscuits as a reward after a hard day at work, why not make love? A gentle hug, pleasure, a hot bath: that's how to reward your efforts! Sex is great for your health, great for your relationship and great for your figure, to be consumed without moderation! It's up to you to make these sexy moments a reality.

⑤ ENDORPHIN: THE HAPPINESS HORMONE

Endorphins are secreted during hard or prolonged physical exercise, like jogging or swimming. It's a powerful pain reliever which brings about a state of wellbeing throughout the whole body. If you make love, make the pleasure last. The longer you last, the more endorphins will be released, to anesthetise your mental state for several hours. You won't need to snack or fill your stomach. Endorphins make the simple act of being a real pleasure.

In the west we make love because of love. Sex is strongly linked to feelings. In the East, their view of sexual relations is very different. Sexual relations in the East have an almost medical function. So in China, making love is seen as a way of caring for the body. So sex is necessary without the need for feelings or desires. The important thing is to do it to ensure the longevity of partners, a different way of looking at things which I'll leave you to ponder.

STAGE 6:

KNOW THE TRUTH ABOUT FOOD

DISCOVER THE TRUTH
ABOUT FOOD

We live in a hyper complex world in which we have to face numerous challenges on a daily basis. We are seriously short of time, and this shortage of time explains why most of us have left it up to others to choose the contents of our plates, these people being supermarkets and the major industrial brands. We trust them firstly because we haven't got the time to check everything, but also because they've managed to create an affective relationship with us, since our childhood.

Think about your favourite foods. Among these foods, how many are raw, of natural origin, and how many are creations of the major brands of the agro-food industry? Recall the images you see and the emotions you feel when thinking about these foods. I'd be willing to bet that they're funny images and pleasant memories. Now think about the phrases that come to mind when you think about these foods. I'm almost certain that they are advertising slogans which you've heard thousands of times since your birth.

When you were little, you understood nothing of the world. When adults plop you in front of the TV for the first time, you don't ask yourself questions. You watch a cartoon. It amuses you and gives you pleasure. As you're brand new and defenceless, you're very impressionable.

This is what the marketing men of the agro-food industry do. As in Perrault's famous tale, the wolf dresses in sheep's clothing to enter your house, in this case to get into your mind.

Most of what we know about food comes from what market men would have us believe. These depictions are wrong or biased simply because they serve the interests of companies who are not interested in informing you but rather making more and more profits. So these depictions are dangerous for your health and that of your family. They make you adopt bad habits, because they encourage you to eat more and more processed foods.

For years I believed that cereal was great for your health. When I wanted to eat a balanced diet, I used to buy cereal for breakfast. Later, when I became a dad, I bought cereal to give to my daughter. I wanted her to grow up with a healthy diet. I was convinced I was doing the right thing. Except that while nutritionists agree that cereals are good for your health, they're not talking about the cereals sold by the major brands, which are full of sugar which encourages weight gain, diabetes and obesity.

The marketing men have appropriated the words of nutritionists to convince thousands of people to buy their products in the belief that they're diet products, while the opposite is true. It's brilliant! That's what they spend their time doing. When the first campaigns against obesity and being overweight appeared, manufacturers invented light foods. When consumers started to worry about pesticides, they invented organic. Except the foods sold were never diet foods.

Anyone who wants to lose weight and have a diet allowing them to live longer needs to examine their beliefs about food, and change them. We need accurate information so we can make the right choices for us and our loved ones. That's what I propose doing in this chapter, by revealing the 3 truths about modern food. By learning the truth, you yourself will decide to change your diet. You'll lose weight and live longer.

In this chapter you will discover the 3 truths about modern food:

- **Truth n°1: why modern food is so calorie rich, and how you can change your diet to consume fewer calories,**
- **Truth n°2: why modern foods are not really foods but chemistry, and therefore by their very nature toxic for your health,**
- **Truth n°3: finally, why foods don't make you happy, and why eating doesn't equate to happiness.**

The great philosophers recommend, when you want to discover the truth about a subject, "suspending" all your beliefs about that subject. You need to do this when it comes to food if you want your beliefs to evolve. Tell yourself you might have been wrong from the very start; maybe what you know and think about this subject is not entirely true; maybe you can learn things and evolve. Changing your opinion is not easy unless you really want to.

You must want to!

TRUE FACT N°1:
MODERN FOODS ARE HYPER CALORIFIC

> **I don't understand; I'm putting on weight even though I'm eating almost nothing!**

I've often heard my patients complain: I don't understand; I'm putting on weight even though I'm eating almost nothing". Most of the time these people are being completely honest, I'm sure. The problem is that these people don't know the truth about modern foods. Everyone should know this truth. We should teach it to children from nursery, and repeat it constantly from then on to prevent the marketing men telling them the opposite. This truth is that:

MODERN PROCESSED FOODS ARE ALL HYPER CALORIFIC!

A while ago I wandered around a supermarket. I felt like having fun. Walking down an aisle, I came face to face with a display cabinet loaded with chocolate "rocks". You've probably already tried them. They're delicious balls of chocolate covered in crushed nuts and filled with praline. There they were, all alone, isolated, as if waiting for me. All I had to do was pick them up and chew. They were so small, they seemed so inoffensive! A little devil sat on my shoulder and whispered: "Go on! It won't hurt you. Look how small they are. They can't have many calories".

As I was being prudent (I was doing my groceries like a tourist walking along a street in Baghdad), before putting them in my basket I took the time to check the ingredients. Small but hefty!!! When you read a label, you need to realise that the first ingredient is the one the food contains most of. In this case, it was sugar followed by nuts. But my greatest surprise was when I discovered that this tiny ball of chocolate, apparently so inoffensive, actually had over 200 calories!

200 calories means nothing – why not 100 or 1,000. Since I've been helping my patients lose weight, I've invented a new way of measuring the calorie content of food. Calories felt too abstract. That's why I substituted a more evocative measure. Now I count it in hours on the exercise bike. When I see a food, I know exactly how long I'd have to pedal to use all the energy contained in it.

This immediately gives me a specific comparator. So you should know that to burn 200 calories, that is to say enough to assimilate that inoffensive chocolate rock, you'd have to pedal for around 30 minutes at the maximum setting of your exercise bike (at least on mine). That's huge! Not to mention the fact that on my visit to the supermarket I could see myself eating two or three.

Of course, that day I didn't have the slightest desire to spend an hour and a half on my exercise bike. Doing that simple calculation helped me give up that fleeting "pleasure".

The truth is that most people under-estimate the calorific content of these modern foods. And by under-estimating this content we eat too much. You think you're "treating yourself", but in fact in a few seconds you're eating the equivalent of your daily need. Remember that 1,800 calories represents a woman's average calorie needs. Just a few chocolate rocks and that's you done for the day! Unless you're happy to store the excess in the form of fat!

For example:

- A croissant = 450 calories.
- 100g of nuts or peanuts = 700 calories.
- A chocolate bar = 500 calories.
- A serving of brownie = 450 calories.
- 100g of pasta = 350 calories.

What's true for chocolate is also true for fizzy drinks, biscuits, crisps, crackers and alcohol. Other than fruits and vegetables, modern food is full of sugar and fat. You need several hours of intensive sport to work off a simple aperitif among friends. Now you understand why so many people put on weight, while finding it unfair. In fact it's not unfair. It's normal to put on weight when you eat such foods, even occasionally.

The marketing men have managed to make us believe that it's normal to eat sugary cereals at breakfast with a large glass of orange juice, and then that for lunch it's normal to eat a nice big meal with a cream pudding and a square of dark chocolate, and that for dinner it's normal to eat a pizza or oven chips with a chunk of meat right after devouring a plate of cured meats for starters. In short, they've managed to make us believe that it's normal to eat twice our actual daily requirements.

That's why so many people don't understand why they get fat. They think they're behaving normally. And they're right. Except they've been ill-informed, indeed manipulated. They've been ill informed to make them eat the products marketed by big brands. But by eating these dishes, putting on weight is almost unavoidable, particularly given that most people live sedentary lives, meaning they consume fewer and fewer calories.

EQUIVALENCE BETWEEN TIME SPENT ON SPORT AND THE CALORIE CONTENT FOODS

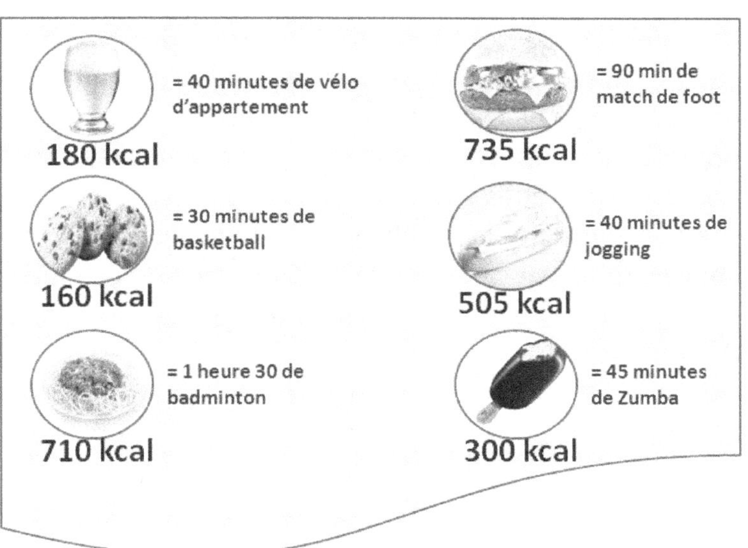

These few examples speak volumes. Suffice to say that if you want to be slim, you have two options. Either do lots of sport, that is to say several hours of sport a day, in which case you can eat whatever you want, or almost. Or you quite simply need to give up a large number of foods which are almost impossible to eat without putting on weight. Here you should be aware that sugary foods are transformed extremely quickly into fat.

The truth is that the manufacturers who produce these foods lie to consumers. They systematically mislead you and do all they can to hide the truth about the products they sell. In truth, these products are not foods, but rather concentrates of sugar and fat! I hope hearing that makes you angry. I hope you realise how much you've been deceived. Do you still feel like buying products from people who lie to you and manipulate you, and voluntarily destroying your health?

It makes me lose my appetite. I have no desire to eat food I know is bad for my health, and which a brand has knowingly lied to me about to make me believe the opposite. It goes against my values. I feel betrayed. I feel angry. If the brands and supermarkets aren't my friends, they're my enemies. When it comes to you, it's your choice. You have the right to continue buying products from people who lie to you and betray you. You can also decide to stop.

It's your choice.

KNOW HOW TO READ LABELS

Examining the ingredients of the foods you buy is an important step in ensuring your health and that of your family. To decide what we want to put on our plate, today it's vital to be able to choose a product according to its ingredients and not its brand, packaging or advertising etc. That's why it's important to be able to decode food labels!

NUTRITIONAL LABELS

Nutritional labels contain information on content in terms of energy and nutrients. Generally it is given for 100g (or 100 ml) of product, and sometimes, in addition, by portion

The mandatory nutritional information is: energy value (in kilocalories – Kcal – and kilojoules – KJ), fats, saturated fatty acids, carbohydrates, sugars, proteins and salt

Other information may be provided on a voluntary basis, such as levels of vitamins and minerals.

WHAT TO LOOK FOR IN THIS INGREDIENT LIST

THE LENGTH OF THE LIST: THE SHORTER THE BETTER!

And for good reason – a long list of ingredients probably means there are a lot of additives or superfluous industrial processes. Above all, look at the end of the list: this is where you'll find the list of additives.

Even if not all additives are toxic, and some are as harmless as vitamin C or E added for preservation purposes, you should nevertheless try and stick to the strict minimum, choosing foods with "simple" compositions.

THE ORDER OF INGREDIENTS:
THIS IS WHAT MAKES THE DIFFERENCE BETWEEN
A HIGH QUALITY PRODUCT AND ANOTHER

Let's take the example of a famous hazelnut spread. When you read the label you notice that hazelnuts appear at the very end of the list of ingredients, while sugar and vegetable oil jostle for first place. In reality, this spread is made of 55% sugar, 23% vegetable oil and just 14% of hazelnuts.

This rule applies to all types of prepared products, savoury or sweet: always check that the ingredients you expect, the ones that would come first to mind if you were making a home-made version, appear first on the list.

THE SUGAR TRAP

5 lumps of sugar is the maximum daily dosage recommended by the WHO (World Health Organisation) for an individual, or 25 grams of sugar a day.

Am I exceeding that limit of five lumps of sugar? To find out, first you need to know the amount of sugar contained in the food you regularly consume. Here are a few examples which show the amount of sugar in some day to day products.

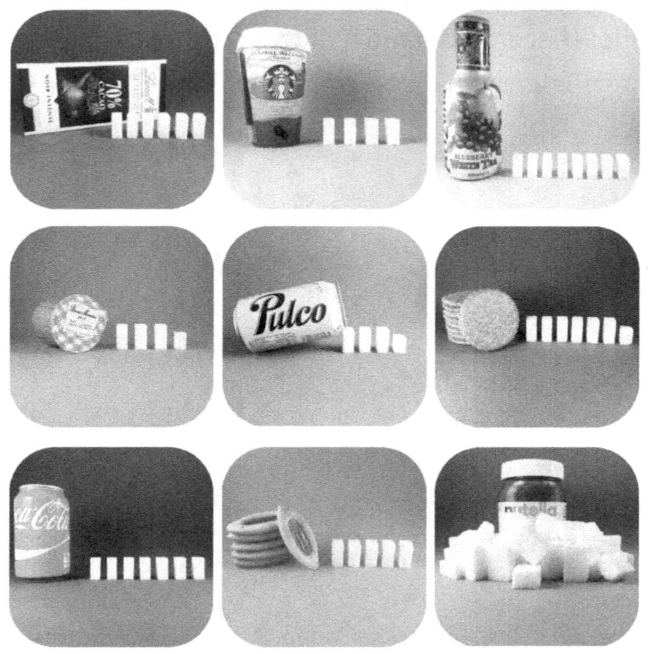

DON'T CONFUSE ORGANIC
AND DIET

The first time I went to an organic grocer's, I was extremely surprised. I was expecting to find healthy, diet foods. What I discovered astounded me. In fact these organic groceries sell the same food as traditional supermarkets. The only difference is that this food comes from organic farms. I'm sure you'll say that makes all the difference. That's very true. But it's not enough. Because eating organic doesn't mean eating well. Let me explain.

Eating organically farmed food is recommended. You avoid ingesting the pollutants present in traditional food, particularly pesticides. Nevertheless, you shouldn't think that organic food is necessarily good for your health. Let me give you an example which shocked me when I visited that organic grocery: I found cereals as full as sugar as the cereals marketed by all the main brands, yet which were supposed to be good for children's health.

These cereals are loaded with sugar and therefore really bad for your health. They are even dangerous in that they encourage weight gain and obesity, and diabetes in later life. Not to mention the fact that these cereals, supposedly intended for breakfast, often end up being devoured in front of the TV in the evening. Sugary cereals are no better for your health than crisps. The same applies to spreads, biscuits and ice cream. An organic pizza is still a pizza.

And it's this confusion I think I should clear up. Organic grocers encourage this confusion to some extent. You go there with the certainty that what you buy will be good for your health. But in fact you're buying foods that aren't good for your health at all. Eating organic food is a plus, but before eating organically you need to learn to eat well, that is to say eating foods that possess the necessary nutritional qualities to ensure good health and avoid weight gain.

Someone who only eats hamburgers, pizzas and ice cream, even organic, will find themselves in a position as dangerous for their health as the same person eating hamburgers, pizzas and ice cream made from conventionally farmed products. So you need to pay attention to the guilt-free effect of organic labels. The most important thing is the nutritional quality of the product rather than its origin and manufacturing method.

Also, traditional supermarkets and the main brands of the agro-food industry encourage this confusion by transforming all traditional foods into organic foods to keep selling them. I'm willing to bet that in less than ten years, 90% of food sold will come from organic farms, yet obesity rates will continue to rise. Keep vigilant and warn your friends and family about this confusion, which is something that needs to be cleared up. While being organic is a plus, in no way does it mean that the food is good for your health.

TRUE FACT N°2:
MOST FOODS
ARE NOT FOODS

The second truth is that most of the foods we eat are not, or are no longer, foods. A vegetable which has grown in a vegetable patch is food. A fruit that has been picked from a tree is food. But food which has undergone numerous transformations through numerous procedures with a host of food additives is no longer food, unless you stretch the definition. The agro-food industry should be renamed the chemical industry to better reflect what it really is.

1 "FAKE FOODS"

The case of the mozzarella you find on cheap pizzas sold in supermarkets is typical. Because in reality this mozzarella isn't cheese! So what is it then? Well, its *lygomme ACH Optimum*, a preparation made of starch, gelling agents and thickeners which replace dairy proteins. This substitution enables savings, as lygomme ACH Optimum costs 60 % less than mass produced cheese and 200% less than actual mozzarella.

The American company Cargill created this "fake cheese" in 2009. While this "fake cheese" contains fewer calories than actual cheese, the truth is it isn't a food in any sense of the word. It's pure chemistry! A brilliant invention created by food scientists working with test tubes. And the case of this "fake cheese" is not an isolated one. Take the case of Surimi, for example. You might think it's crab meat. In fact it's 62% a mixture of oil, starch, sugar, water and artificial flavourings!

② PROCESSED FOODS

The other factor making modern foods more and more chemical is that the methods of processing foods (cooking, treatments, preservatives etc.) used by the industry are more and more complex. They bring about the development of chemical substances inside the foods themselves. Here is a non-exhaustive list of chemical substances you might find in foods after they've been processed. This list is non-exhaustive, and most of these elements are carcinogenic.

- Acrylamide,
- Benzene,
- Chloropropanols,
- Furane,
- Heterocyclic aromatic hydrocarbons,
- Polycyclic aromatic hydrocarbons (PAH),
- Nitrosamine,
- Semi-carbazide,
- Urethane.

Acrylamide is a chemical substance that forms in certain foods while being processed or cooked at a high temperature. Its presence has been detected in many products coming from the agro-food industry. The largest concentrations of this product have been observed in crisps and fried potatoes. If you regularly eat frozen or oven chips, you've probably ingested acrylamide.

Furan can be found in low concentrations in heat-treated food such as preserved or tinned foods. Different procedures can cause furan to form in foods. Due to its toxicity for the liver and the risks of cancer observed among laboratory animals exposed to furan through foods, the presence of furan in foods is a real health risk. The International Agency for Research on Cancer (IARC) has classified it as carcinogenic for humans.

❸ FOOD ADDITIVES

The third factor explaining why modern foods are less and less natural is the use of synthetic food additives. These are added to mass produced food to improve its look, taste and preservation. Their long term effects on health are still little known but some of them are suspected of being toxic and causing side effects such as allergies, illnesses, behavioural problems and even cancers. Here is a list of additives that should be avoided if you want to stay healthy.

ENEMY N°1: GLUCOSE SYROP

Glucose syrup is a sugar concentrate extracted from corn. It causes sudden blood sugar spikes and long term damage to the liver, while increasing the risk of diabetes.

Glucose syrup is present in almost all biscuits but also some cold meats. Manufacturers add it to a lot of food because they've long been aware of the addictive nature of sugar. Put another way, they know that glucose syrup will, sub-consciously, make you want to eat their products.

ENEMY N°2: ARTIFICIAL COLOURING

Migraines, sight problems and also behavioural problems among children…the consumption of high doses of food colourings is toxic for your health. Represented by codes E100 to E199, they are almost everywhere, particularly sweets. They attract and seduce the consumer with their appetising colours, in many cases hiding the poor quality of the product sold. Manufacturers excel in the art of improving the look of a product to the detriment of its nutritional qualities.

ENEMY N°3: ARTIFICIAL SWEETENERS

Artificial sweeteners are as bad for your health as sugar! Without any studies proving it, today they are nevertheless suspected of causing certain illnesses. Sweeteners cause a dependency on sugary foods and can help cause diabetes. They are found in most light foods.

ENEMY N°4: PARTIALLY HYDROGENATED OILS OR TRANSFATTY ACIDS

These are oils made solid or semi-solid and then put into foods to replace more expensive butter. They can be found in almost all mass produced pastries and cakes! They increase rates of "bad cholesterol" and reduce rates of "good cholesterol". What better way to block arteries and cause heart attacks?

ENEMY N°5: BUTYLATED HYDROXYTOLUENE

This synthetic additive is used as an antioxidant. Its use is controversial. It can cause allergies and even cancer and could also be responsible for increasing cholesterol. It is indicated by code E321. A chemical product is never neutral when found in food.

ENEMY N°6: NITRATES

Nitrates are additives present in processed meats to extend their conservation and give them an appetising pink colour. It has recently been proven that consuming too much of this additive increases the risk of cancer of the stomach and intestine.

ENEMY N°7: SODIUM BENZOATE

Sodium benzoate is used as a preservative. It is suspected of causing hyperactivity in children when combined with other additives like colouring. Sodium benzoate, combined with vitamin C (ascorbic acid) turns into benzene, a highly carcinogenic compound.

THE TOP 5 FOODS TO AVOID TO STAY HEALTHY

If you want to lose weight and live longer, there are some foods you should decide to give up. Don't give them up because your doctor asks you to, or because you decide to go on a diet, give them up because you are aware, because in your heart of hearts you know these foods are bad for you. You don't want to eat bad things anymore, because, quite simply, you have self-respect.

① CRISPS

Crisps are 70% oil, 25% potatoes and 5% food additives and salt. There's nothing worse for your weight, wellbeing and health. If you want to be depressed, feel bad and destroy your health, eat crisps. Otherwise, cut them out.

② SAUCES

Sauces like mayonnaise and cream-based sauces are very rich in saturated fats. These sauces will make your cholesterol rate rocket. Also, they have no nutritional value. In short, they aren't foods!

③ PROCESSED MEATS

Processed meats are extremely fatty. Think about all those white spots in sausage, which are all small pieces of fat. Why eat so much fat, storing up so many problems for yourself?

④ PASTRIES

Croissants, pain au chocolate or raison bread are celebratory foods! But they're nothing more than sugar and fat (butter but more commonly hydrogenated margarine...). So this type of food is really not a good way to start your day.

⑤ FIZZY DRINKS

Fizzy drinks are just a clever mix of sugars and chemical products. We drink them cold because they're so sugary that they're hard to drink at room temperature. Try drinking a couple of glasses at room temperature to see how disgusting they are!

TRUE FACT N°3: FOOD DOESN'T MAKE YOU HAPPY

The marketing men manipulate our emotions and desires by associating images of happy people with the foods they want to sell, making us sub-consciously confuse happiness and food!

Take a few seconds to think about all the food adverts you've seen since your childhood. Remember the happy faces of those families sharing a tasty pizza, the delicious curves of those pretty young women, lying in suggestive poses and enjoying a vanilla cream or a yoghurt etc. Joy, friendship, love, sex, adventure – the marketing men know the art of associating simple foods with the perfect scenes we'd all like to have really experienced.

But the marketing men are not solely to blame. Since you were a child, most important moments with friends and family have involved food. French culture is almost unique in the importance it places on food. Food is at the heart of human relationships. It's impossible to meet friends or family without the event turning into lunch, dinner, a picnic, barbecue or aperitif.

An ordinary wedding

A short while ago I went to the wedding of one of my best friends. It was a lovely autumn day and a lovely wedding. Everything, from the town hall to the dancing in the evening, was perfect.

As I drove home the following afternoon, I started to think. I'd just stopped eating and, drunk with tiredness, I was in a hurry to get home and rest.
I had a horrible migraine from too much sparkling wine and pains in my muscles and liver.

The truth is, there's no good reason to make yourself sick while celebrating a happy event. Why drink alcohol whenever something good or interesting happens in your life? Why make yourself ill when something great and wonderful happens. It's strange. The body is capable of bringing us so much wellbeing and satisfaction that it's really a shame to deprive it of this capacity at such an important and positive moment.

You should understand one thing, and this will set you free: other people aren't always right. Just because most French people behave like this doesn't mean it's the right way to behave. Now when I go to a wedding I don't drink alcohol and eat very little. In this way I enjoy my evening but also the next day, and I tell myself I can make the most of each day of my life in that way, feeling comfortable in my body.

What I in fact realised was that eating and drinking will never make me happy. These are ephemeral pleasures at best. On the contrary, when you've eaten, you want to go to sleep. When you've drunk too much, your behaviour can become extreme. Some people get depressed and others aggressive. Then, for several days you feel uncomfortable in your skin. Eating or drinking too much cuts us off from our body. But what is worse, we're destroying our health. If you respect yourself you should refuse to behave like this, because you just need to preserve the life you have.

When you become aware of all that, it's not difficult to say "NO THANKS" to a relative or friend who offers you a glass of alcohol. It's an assured and benevolent "NO THANKS" which has its roots in the deepest part of ourselves, in our desire for self-preservation. By saying "NO THANKS", you're merely protecting yourself as you would naturally protect yourself from any danger. You leave it up to others to behave how they like, but you just demand the right to have your different choices respected.

DOES A BALANCED DIET MAKE YOU HAPPY? EXPERT SCIENTIFIC OPINION

Numerous scientific studies have shown the direct link between food, brain function and behaviour. Despite the large amount of data available, the authorities have largely failed to follow up on this with actual recommendations.

Yet with the development of medical imaging techniques, researchers are able to identify molecules in our food that can influence hormones and neuro-transmitters, and therefore our behaviour. We are what we eat!

Here I will present a few studies which demonstrate this link. Scary!

1 SOME FOODS MAKE YOU AGGRESSIVE

In a study carried out in a prison environment, Gesch et Al (2002) administered food supplements consisting, among others, of fatty acids and vitamins to 231 prisoners. Results showed that those who had received these food supplements committed 25% fewer acts of violence and that their aggression levels after two weeks on this diet had fallen 35% compared with those who had received a placebo.

David Hemenway, from Harvard Public Health School, interviewed almost 1900 teenagers between 14 and 18 in the Boston area about their eating habits and certain violent acts, for example taking a weapon to school, being violent to their peers, family members or girlfriend or boyfriend.

The results indicated that among those who consumed **a can of sugary drink** a week:

- 23% had brought a weapon to school,
- 15% had been violent towards their partner in the year leading up to the survey,
- 35% had been violent to their peers during the same period.
- Among those who consumed **14 cans a week:**
- 43% had brought a knife or gun to school,
- 27% had been violent towards a partner, and
- 58% towards their peers.

The various socio-economic factors that could influence the result (family situation, parental attitudes, intellectual quotient) were taken into account.

Finally, in a famous study carried out in a high school in Wisconsin USA, the re-balancing of meals brought spectacular results. On the menu were natural proteins, whole cereals, fruits and vegetables, all prepared on site without colouring, preservatives, fries or fizzy drinks. The result: the kids were more disciplined, more focused and had better grades. Just changing pupils' diet had a huge impact on their behaviour.

These first three studies show that mass produced food rich in fat, sugar and additives, can have an extremely negative impact on mood, emptions and behaviour. Conversely, adopting a balanced diet rich in fatty acids and vitamins can reduce aggressive and anti-social behaviour. Put another way, mass produced food increases stress and negative emotions. It makes people tense.

This means that by changing your diet, you can be less stressed, suffer less from mood swings and experience fewer negative emotions. This means you can reduce the number and intensity of conflicts (work, family partner, etc.) you might otherwise have with others. Yet conflicts play an extremely important role in the quality of life. By choosing to change your diet for good, you're choosing to enter a virtuous circle which boosts your personal wellbeing and encourages harmonious relationships with others.

② SOME FOOD ADDITIVES INCREASE HYPERACTIVITY AMONG CHILDREN

A study by McCann et Al (2007) showed that the consumption of 6 artificial colourings and a preservative contained in sweets and some drinks could increase hyperactivity among children. Put another way, the consumption of food additives could cause behavioural problems.

③ SOME FOODS INCREASE THE RISK OF DEPRESSION

An important study by Akbaraly, Brunner et al (2009) resulted from the study of 3,426 people over five years. Separated into two groups, they had two different diets, one rich in fried and processed foods, the others based on a Mediterranean style diet, rich in vegetables, fruits and fish.

The findings were unequivocal: **a diet rich in processed foods increases by the risk of depression by 58% compared with a normal diet;** whereas the consumption of vegetables, fruits and fish increases the same risk by 26%. Antioxidants, polyphenols and polyunsaturated fatty acids, but also omega-3 and probiotics seem to play a role in depression. A lack of them increases the risk, while eating enough reduces it.

THE TRUTH ABOUT STRICT DIETS

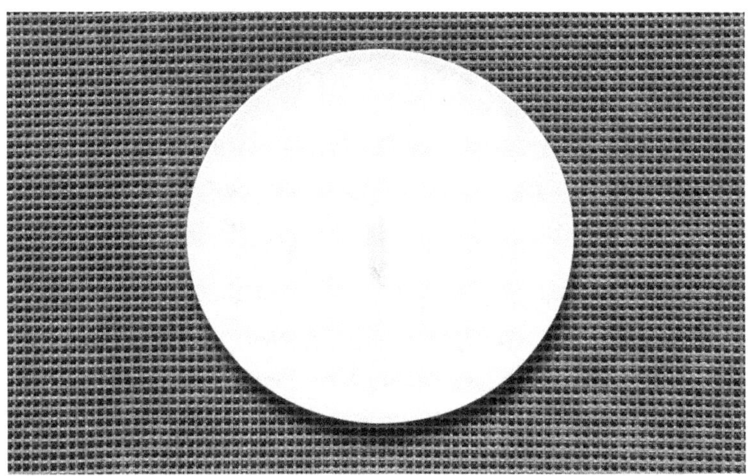

In the United States, a famous reality show, "The Biggest Loser", invites overweight people to go on a very strict diet to lose weight. The winner is the one who loses the higher percentage of his weight compared with the beginning of the show. The results are spectacular, as evidenced by the story of Danny, who went from 195 to 86 kg (429 to 180 lbs.), or a loss of 109 kg (240 lbs.) between the start of the show and the day of the finale. For this he won the tidy sum of 250,000 dollars.

Specialist researchers in obesity, who publish their results in the *Obesity* review, monitored the participants in this show for 6 years after their weight loss. Here are their conclusions. Their observations shed light on the consequences of a strict diet and losing weight too quickly. For any readers who've already been on a strict diet, the results should help you better understand the famous "yoyo" effect and why it is so difficult to maintain weight loss in the long term.

① A DECREASED METABOLISM

Six years after the broadcast, Danny weighed 133 kg. (293 lbs.). Like thirteen out of the fourteen participants in the show, he had put weight back on in the years following it. Four participants even weighed more than they had before the show. According to the researchers who conducted this study, the explanation is the following: after an excessively strict diet, the body sets to regaining all the kilos lost through a specific metabolic mechanism. There is a decrease in the metabolism, that is to say the number of calories consumed naturally by the body.

Thus they discovered that at rest, Danny's body was using up 800 calories less than a man of the same age and the same weight. His metabolism had slowed down. Several years later, it was preventing him from losing weight, by storing fat and burning the fewest calories possible, in order to return to its original weight. It's almost as if the body had been programed to reach this weight. It's as if the fact of being forced to lose too much weight too quickly had had the opposite effect.

According to the researchers who conducted this study, this mechanism can also be explained by a fall in the rate of leptin, the fullness hormone, which regulates hunger, in the blood of participants. At the end of the show, all participants had very low leptin levels. They had lost weight but were almost always hungry because of the lack of this hormone. Over the years, levels climbed again but never reached the levels recorded before the show.

The conclusions of this study fully support our method, which aims for gradual weight lose while changing your lifestyle for good. With our method, you'll never lose the weight lost simply because you'll never eat overly fatty or sugary foods again. They will have simply disappeared from your diet because that's the decision you made. Going on a strict diet is pointless; you need to change the way you eat and live for good.

STAGE 7:
BEATING YOUR ADDICTIONS

BEAT YOUR ADDICTIONS

Gambling, drugs, alcohol, the Internet, endurance or extreme sports, work or food, addictions can affect anybody, any time, any place. Addictions consist of the repetition of an action that you can't stop yourself from doing. People who suffer from an addiction often say:

"IT'S STRONGER THAN ME!"
OR "I CAN'T STOP MYSELF".

They might realise that their behaviour is harmful. They might want to stop but be unable to do so.

In this case, people have the impression that they are constantly fighting themselves. This "fight" is exhausting. And when they no longer have the resources to control their behaviour, it's called a "relapse". For example this is what happens when an alcoholic who has been able to stay dry for several days, suddenly falls off the wagon, or when someone who is addicted to food suddenly binge eats. We call this bulimia.

Addictions are characterised by two main things:

- **The behaviour lasts a long time:** we talk of an addiction when someone is unable to stop their behaviour for several months, indeed years. Some addictions can also last a lifetime.

- **The increase in the frequency and scale of the behaviour:** if we're talking about drugs, people increase their "doses" and "consume" them more and more frequently, If we're talking about an action, they will tend to repeat it more and more frequently and in an increasingly extreme manner.

In the case of a gambling addiction for example, people will gamble more and more frequently, betting more and more money to the point of ruining themselves. If someone is taking a drug, they will increase their doses and the frequency until they risk overdosing. If the person is a food addict, they'll tend to eat more and more often, in ever greater quantities, obviously leading to serious health issues.

THE WRONG RESPONSE TO A REAL NEED

Behind every addiction is a real need. The person needs something. To meet this need, they adopt certain behaviour or consume a product. The problem is that very often the product does not meet that person's real needs. For example, the person might be suffering from anxiety. To reduce their anxiety, they start drinking alcohol. Alcohol effectively reduces their anxiety but fails to treat the cause of anxiety. The real need is a solution to the person's anxiety.

That's why, all too often the product or behaviour progressively loses its effectiveness, and why people increase doses in response to this loss of effectiveness. Not only does the body get used to it, but the person also adopts the wrong response to their problem. If, in the above case, we admit that anxiety is linked to job insecurity, alcohol will definitely not be the right response, and nor will it improve the person's sense of security.

And when it comes to food, it works in exactly the same way. Some people eat too often and too much. They use food to meet some of their needs: receiving love, feeling pleasure, relaxing or comforting themselves... Except food is not the right response to these real needs. That's why, once the bar of chocolate has been devoured, they continue to feel the same malaise, the same sense of emptiness, added to which they have a feeling of guilt.

Jeanne's separation

Jeanne is a patient on our diet hypnosis program. She came to us because she'd been suffering from a chocolate addiction for several months. She eats too much chocolate and can'tstop. She can eat up to 3 bars a day. Often it is in the evening, while watching TV, that she has her "crises".

While she always used to eat chocolate, a chunk from time to time at most, her consumption really started to become a problem when she separated from her husband, who she'd lived with for 5 years. This was a few weeks ago. He left her because they were always arguing.

Jeanne has a 5 year old boy, and she immediately raised her concerns for the future. She doesn't know what they're going to do about the custody of their son. She's worried that her husband could move, find a new partner, avoid paying alimony; particularly given that he was the main breadwinner.

Jeanne founded her company just a year ago. I could tell she was very anxious. I immediately understood that Jeanne was using chocolate as an anxiolytic. Food has this type of calming property when it is consumed in large quantities. I realised that Jeanne needed security.
In your opinion, can chocolate provide her with security?

The work we carry out with Jeanne bears on 3 subjects:

Firstly I want to teach her how to better manage her anxiety by accepting her reality and focusing on the here and now. The future is nothing more than uncertainty. Thinking too much about the future is often a source of worry. There are so many possibilities that it's impossible to guess what will happen. It's pointless to consider each and every possible scenario.

Then I want to change the way she perceives chocolate, which isn't a food, no matter what people

Once addiction takes hold, the true need is hidden. The person is so focused on the problem of their addiction that they're no longer thinking about their actual problem and how to resolve it. That's why so many people find it hard to quit an addiction, simply because when the addiction comes to an end, the real problem resurfaces. Then the person needs to confront their real problems and take action which is not always easy.

In Jeanne's case, she is focused on her chocolate addiction. And that's why she chose to consult a therapist. Yet chocolate isn't her real problem. Her real problem is the issue of her financial independence after her separation. She needs to take action, and is sure she'll fail. That's why she's focused on her addiction. An addiction is a way of diverting your attention from your real problem by creating another problem which appears easier to solve

ACTION N°1:
GET USED TO "WATCHING THE WHOLE FILM"

To fight an addiction, first you need to change your relationship with the food consumed. Doctor Benhaiem, a French hypnosis specialist, who trained me in the treatment of patients suffering from food addictions, suggests an extremely interesting technique. For doctor Benhaiem, the patient needs to "watch the whole film". "Watching the whole film" means understanding and physically feeling all the causes and consequences of eating this food.

Imagine a person suffering from an addiction to a famous chocolate spread. When this person eats chocolate spread they're focused on the here and now. They only perceive the sensation of chocolate in their mouth. When performing this act, they are focussed solely on this action and this sensation. It's a kind of tunnel vision that ignores the causes and consequences of their actions. If they want to reduce their addiction, they need to go back in time, to the origins of this spread, and go into the future to see the consequences of this action.

I suggest together we write the script of a film that depicts the consumption of a teaspoon of chocolate spread. To do so, first we need to go back to the origins of this chocolate spread. This chocolate spread comes from a distant country. It comes from a palm oil plantation. This plantation was created by burning a forest and killing all the animals that lived there. On this plantation, men women and children work hard to earn a pittance. The region is devastated by fire and pollution.

Once the fruits of the palm tree are harvested, they are transported to a large factory. In this factory, they are transformed into palm oil, which is then mixed with sugar, nuts and cocoa, to create a chocolate spread by following a special recipe. So this spread mainly consists of fat and sugar. Then additives are added to preserve it, and artificial flavourings to further improve the taste and its addictive power. The aim of these manufacturers is to sell as much of this chocolate spread as possible.

Now imagining the marketing department of this company which sells chocolate spread around the world, and has to create attractive adverts to convince you to eat more of this food. Imagine the shareholders of this company who have agreed on the guidelines and strategy to get consumers, especially children, who are their main target, to eat more and more of this food. A child potentially has 70 years of consumption ahead of them. And children are more sensitive to the influence of advertising.

They are well aware of the fact that this food is bad for your health, that it will make thousands of children obese, and years later cause cardio-vascular problems, morbid obesity and all sorts of suffering. But they laugh it off. Think about those shareholders, those directors, those marketing people. To grow their business, they set about transforming a poison into a "happy food". These people are totally indifferent to your fate because they despise you.

Now think about those products stacked on the shelves of your regular supermarket. Imagine walking down the street watching the telly or surfing the Internet, constantly bombarded with advertising messages, to the point you believe that this spread is indeed a happy food. Sub-consciously you feel the desire to buy this chocolate spread because like many human beings, you just want to be happy, and are seeking ways of achieving it.

You've seen the first part of the film. And now comes the second part.

Now imagine you're eating this chocolate spread. Feel the taste in your mouth: the palm oil, the sugar, the nuts, the cocoa, the food additives. Perhaps you find it delicious. Except you're not only eating a chocolate spread. You're eating a devastated forest. Thousands of dead trees and animals. You're eating the scorn and cynicism of the people running that company. What you're eating is a product full of fat and sugar. What you're eating is death.

You feel the taste of this chocolate spread which flatters your palate and you feel it enter your stomach like glue. This paste has been designed to arouse your brain by flooding your blood with fat and sugar and creating dependency. Tobacco makers used the same strategies to get smokers hooked on nicotine. Except today, sugar kills more people than cigarettes. And it is a cruel murderer of nice people who eat without considering the harm they are doing to themselves.

Now imagine where this fat and sugar goes. It is stored directly in the form of fat. It transforms into plaque which blocks your arteries. After eating breakfast, sugar creates glycaemic peaks which causes mood swings and makes you aggressive, not to mention its devastating effect on your live. This so-called "happy food" is killing you softly, teaspoon by teaspoon. It's a slow but deadly poison that you were stupid enough to buy, placing your trust in liars.

The worst is that once you've eaten that spread, once the first sensations of pleasure have dissipated, you start feeling uncomfortable in your skin. You feel heavy. You're flooded with negative thoughts and a feeling of heaviness. You're ashamed because you know you're already over weight and you should never have eaten that hyper-calorific food. You blame yourself for giving in to temptation yet again. You feel terrible, caught in a trap.

You thought it would make you happy, but in the end it just makes you unhappy. And this feeling doesn't go away. It comes back every time you get on the scales, try on a pair of trousers that don't fit, when you feel the extra fat on your abdomen, your thighs and buttocks. Because that's the toxic waste from that chocolate spread is stored, often for years. For just a few seconds of sweet taste on your tongue, you'll suffer for years.

And then one day, something pops in your brain. Your arteries, blocked by consuming that paste, have become fragile. One moment there you were, calm, chatting. You fall to the ground. You wake up several hours later. You can't speak properly. Your doctor says you'll never talk properly again. You find it hard to walk. Your memory no longer functions properly. Part of your brain has died after this stroke. You've become disabled, and it's irreversible.

And for this you have the well-known make of chocolate spread which sold you the food of happiness. And that's that, you know the consequences. The end! You've watched the whole film. By watching the whole film you realise that this spread isn't designed to make you happy. For 5 seconds of happiness, several years of malaise. And this idea stays with you. If you were about to treat yourself to a little spoonful of chocolate spread, you put it to one side. You take the jar and just throw it in the bin.

ACTION N°2: MAKE A DIRECT CONNECTION TO YOUR MEMORY

Stéphanie and the pastries

Stéphanie is a patient who came to me suffering from an addiction to pastries. Whenever she passed by a famous local patisserie, she was unable to resist. She would stop, buy a pastry and treat herself. Of course, this meant she put on weight. So she wanted to lose this addiction.

I spent a long time discussing this with Stéphanie. She told me that when she ate a pastry, it reminded her of the special moments she had spent with her grandmother when she was little. Her grandmother would always make delicious Alsatian cakes for her. Stéphanie is originally from Alsace, and had moved to Paris for work.

As we talked, we discovered that eating cakes was simply a way for Stéphanie to reconnect with her memories, with her happy times spent in the village of her birth, with her grandmother who was a generous person she loved a lot. Stéphanie was connecting to a moment of her life, a beloved person.

Cakes were like the "play" button of a DVD containing all the happy memories of her childhood. By eating a cake, she was watching the images again, feeling emotions, diving back into her memories. Her body was remembering. Each time, she felt a great feeling of relaxation and comfort.

Her addiction had its origin in Stephanie's attempt to relive her lost memories. That's why she was unable to quit. Simply because she was unable to give up the love of her grandmother she missed so much, and that link with her home country which she carried in her heart, and for which she felt so much nostalgia.

Once we had found the cause, it was easy to get rid of the addiction.

Indeed, all it took (which is what I would do) was to show Stéphanie that she could reconnect with her memories and the pleasant emotions that were linked to them, merely by thinking about them. And she didn't need pastries to do so. She just needed to take five minutes, close her eyes and recall her childhood memories. It's like a moment of contemplation. A moment in which we can remember the best moments of our life, the people who have loved us, the times we received love and when we felt good.

The body has a memory. In this memory are stored all the states it has experienced over its life: states of happiness as well as suffering. And it's possible to reactivate this memory through the power of thought alone. The body thus returns to a former state. When Stéphanie ate cakes with her grandmother, she felt calm, protected and loved. If she makes the effort to remember, her body returns to exactly the same state, and she feels calm, protected and loved again, even though her grandmother isn't there.

If you suffer from a food addiction, you should do this exercise. Remember the day you started eating that food. Remember all the times that food was present in your life. Remember your emotions at these times. Remember who was present. Eating can help you bring back someone you've lost, an emotion you no longer experience, transport you to a state which no longer exists. This is the "Madeleine de Proust" effect.

Get into the habit of taking a few minutes out of each day to "contemplate". Close your eyes and think of these memories. Let the emotions, sensations and images come to you. Concentrate, trying to recall each detail: the images, sounds, smells, tastes and sensations...Then you will see something extraordinary happening within you. As if by magic, your body returns to its state at that precise moment. The body's memory is as powerful as the mind's.

If you do this with memories linked to food, you'll see that your addiction to this food disappears immediately. Because you've discovered that you don't need this food to bring back that lovely memory you were seeking. What

I propose here is merely a short cut, a more direct route to what you were really seeking through your addiction. Trust in the power of the body and the mind. Take this path and your addiction will disappear. I have personal experience of this.

We live in a time when most rituals have disappeared. We don't contemplate any more. We no longer remember. We no longer take the time to stop and think about important and essential things such as people we've lost. And here I'm not talking about nostalgia or sadness. Thinking about someone you've lost in this way would be totally counterproductive. The aim is not to feel regret or remorse. The aim is to reconnect to a moment in your life in a peaceful and joyous way, to relive a precious moment.

This might seem out of fashion in the age of materialism. Yet I'm convinced we need these moments to be happy. This is something I've discovered as I've grown older, and feel I've gained a great deal through this realisation. Learn to do nothing but connect yourself to your past. Act as if you were still living those moments. You will see a great improvement in your life. Your addictions will disappear and you will regain your power over your life.

EXERCISE: THE MAGICAL RESTAURANT

① OBJECTIVES

One day my 3 year old daughter invited me to play a game. Her game was called: the restaurant. At the time I was doing a GLE diet (gluten, lactose and egg-free). I'd stopped eating many foods that I used to enjoy, including cakes and puddings. I accepted with grace and sat at a small table in her bedroom. The game began. And what was on offer was really delicious: chocolate cake, custard, profiteroles, choux buns, my little chef brought me everything I ordered. I indulged myself for over an hour, to the point that it was she who, tired by the game, had to throw me out of her "restaurant". That was when I realised we could enjoy the pleasure of eating without eating. And that's how the "Magical restaurant" came to be.

A lot of people put on weight because they eat too much in the evening or after a difficult day at work full of tension and stress. They want to treat themselves by eating fatty and calorie filled foods. It's a reward for their efforts. What they really want is not food but the pleasure that food gives them. This pleasure brings about peace of mind, comfort, relaxation. It acts as a reward for all their efforts. The principle of this concept is to allow patients to access pleasure directly through the mere power of the mind. By imagining that you eat, your brain secretes, as if by magic, the same neuro-transmitters as if you were really eating.

② SEQUENCE

Get comfortable, close your eyes and focus on your breathing. Gradually you achieve a state of relaxation.

Imagine that you're transported to the doors of a restaurant anywhere on Earth, where they offer you the best dishes in the world, created by an excellent chef.

You're starving. You enter the restaurant. You perceive its décor, its atmosphere. The host greets you.

You can order any dish you want and as much as you wish, in the order you wish. You decide to order your favourite dish.

You bring the food to your mouth, and have never tasted anything as nice.

Each mouthful is a delight. The tastes are perfect, as is the temperature and the seasoning.

You indulge in this dish, and when it's gone you can order it again or try another dish. You feel the infinite pleasure of eating anything you want.

You feel light, as these dishes don't fill your stomach. Happy, you leave the restaurant in the knowledge that somewhere there's a place you can return to when you want, just by using your imagination.

ACTION N°3: CHANGE THE WAY YOU PERCEIVE FOOD

When you suffer from a food addiction, this addiction is often linked to the way you perceive that food. For example, you see all sorts of positive and attractive things in a fizzy drink. And it's the marketing men, as we've seen all too often, who are partially responsible for the way you perceive this food. Sometimes this is all sub-conscious. They are even, and most commonly, unconscious. That's why they have such an influence on your habits and your behaviour. They influence you without you being aware of it.

Let's take the example of a famous cola. I conducted a survey on social media. I asked Internet users to give me the 5 words that immediately came to mind when they heard the name of that famous soft drink. These were the most common answers:

Negative words	Positive words
• Sugar,	• Cool,
• Obesity,	• Celebration,
• Agent,	• Freshness,
• Multi-national,	• Energy,
• Unhealthy,	• Friends,
• Addiction,	• Aperitif,
• Danger.	• Excitement.

Source: survey conducted among 800 Internet users between 1 and 8 May 2016

Internet users are aware of the risks related to regular consumption of fizzy drinks, because of their high levels of sugar and caffeine, which makes it a highly addictive product. They understood that the consumption of this drink was linked to mass advertising campaigns, behind which was a multi-national with huge powers. Also, most of them mentioned these words first, a sign that they are well informed of the public health problems arising from the consumption of this drink.

But, paradoxically, when asked if they drank it, most of them answered in the affirmative. As with tobacco, people are aware of the dangers of fizzy drinks but continue to drink them. To properly understand what's going on, you need to look at the context and moments linked to the consumption of this drink. For this, you need to look at the positive words cited by Internet users. They mainly evoke moments of celebration, enjoyable times with friends.

This is linked to the fact that fizzy drinks are seen as the perfect drink for children's parties. It's the "alcohol of kids". When an adult wants to celebrate something in France, they drink a glass of champagne or sparkling wine. When you're a kid, you have a fizzy drink. Later, when you're a teenager you mix these fizzy drinks with alcohol to make their consumption more fun. Bubbles somehow connote lightness, happiness and the joy inherent to all celebrations.

But behind the words are the events and memories that Internet users associate with this fizzy drink. They recall a birthday meal, a party, a student night...Fizzy drinks recall happy moments of their lives, which they will probably never relive. Sub-consciously, the affective link with fizzy drinks is extremely powerful. To some extent, whenever the person drinks that drink, they immediately relive all the happy moments they have experienced with it in the past.

The day that person decides to stop drinking this fizzy drink because it's bad for their health (by the way, there's nothing worse than that drink...), they'll have the feeling (no doubt sub-conscious) of having to make a break with all that, as if by giving up this fizzy drink, they are also giving up the chance of partying with friends. And that's where the addictive power of a food lies, in its meaning, developed over years, through a person's history, sometimes an entire lifetime.

If you make a parallel with a drug like cannabis, it's not the cannabis itself that creates this addiction but everything associated with it. Someone who smokes it feels different. They feel cool, rebellious...It makes them think of Baudelaire, Bob Marley or Bob Dylan in the 70s... Cannabis makes them dream, and when they smoke, they live that dream. They fantasise, consciously or sub-consciously, of being Baudelaire, Bob Marley or Bob Dylan. It makes them live a powerful experience. And the day they stop smoking, they have to give that fantasy up.

However, it's clear that this is all just an illusion. Giving up fizzy drinks will never stop you partying with your friends, in the same way as smoking cannabis will never stop you being a cool and rebellious person. So to limit your addiction you need to profoundly change your sub-conscious perception of food. By changing this perception, you'll lose your desire for this food as if by magic. The irresistible attraction you felt will become indifference, even ejection.

To profoundly change your perception of the food you're addicted to, you need to provide your brain with new information, new information that will replace what you used to think, and bring about disgust, rejection or indifference to this food. This new information can be conveyed in the form of stories or suggestions. In the hypnosis sessions we give, we bring about this type of change in perception.

Here are a few stories to read that might help you reduce your addictions to certain foods.

A TALE TO STOP YOU EATING CHOCOLATE

The secrets behind the making of chocolate

Did you know that chocolate is made of cocoa?

Cocoa beans are harvested from a tree which grows in South America, which is called the cacao tree.

When they are harvested, the beans are so small that they are gathered alongside twigs and leaves.

And many small creatures live on these twigs and leaves: there are worms, cockroaches, flies, aphids, grasshoppers, slugs, caterpillars, spiders and their eggs.

The cocoa beans, the cuttings and insects are then stored in a large warehouse so they can dry.

It's all sprayed with chemical products to kill all the animals, but the eggs survive. It's so difficult to separate the twigs and dead insects from the cocoa beans that it's all crushed up together.

All the insects: the worms, the cockroaches, the flies, the aphids, the grasshoppers, slugs, caterpillars, spiders and their eggs are mixed up with the cocoa beans.

This means that when you're eating chocolate, you're actually eating not only cocoa beans but also worms, cockroaches, flies, aphids, grasshoppers, slugs, caterpillars and spiders.

And above all you're eating their eggs, which can hatch in your stomach when you eat chocolate.

Think about this the next time you fancy a bar of chocolate. Think about the fact that hidden within those lovely chocolate bars are the bodies of worms, cockroaches, caterpillars, flies, slugs and spiders.

And if you have a stomach ache after eating it, tell yourself it could be a spider's egg hatching in your stomach, and a large spider with hairy legs is hatching and growing in your entrails.

A TALE TO STOP YOU EATING FAST FOOD

Meow, Meow

Did you know that employees of fast food restaurant are under huge time pressures and often ignore basic rules of hygiene, such as washing their hands after going to the toilet?

They scratch their oily hair before touching the bread. They sneeze over hamburgers, leaving them covered with mucus which is then covered by sauce.

Analyses of hamburgers and fries carried out by specialist laboratories have revealed the presence of faecal bacteria, flu viruses and traces of human sebum in hamburger meat.

And on several occasions it has been found that hamburgers contain more than beef. For example, one day a man choked on a small piece of bone which was hidden in a hamburger. The bone could have killed him by getting stuck in his throat. Later the small piece of bone was analysed.

It was discovered that the bone came from a rat whose meat had been mixed with the beef. The fast food chain was supplied with meat from a factory which killed the rats and added them to the meat.

To save money, some manufacturers have even been found guilty of mixing horse meat with beef. But the worst is that some analyses have revealed the presence of cat and dog meat.

Often animal pounds, to get rid of euthanized cats and dogs, sell them on to hamburger makers. They know that nobody will detect this deception because of the taste of the sauce which hides the taste of the meat.

The next time you go to a fast food restaurant and bite into your burger, remember there could be a bit of rat or cat inside. Think about this when stuffing your face with a hamburger dripping in sauce.

Imagine a cat crying "meow meow" at each mouthful.

That might make you lose your appetite...

A TALE TO STOP YOU EATING SWEETS

The true history of sweets

Imagine pretty sweets of every colour, the pretty sweets you would love to eat and maybe even give to children.

But do you know precisely how sweets are made?

Did you know the main ingredient of sweets is pork gelatine?

Yes, but what exactly is pork gelatine?

To answer this question, just imagine a nice pink pig. It's just like the one in the story of the three little pigs you read as a child. Maybe you still read it to your children or grandchildren.

Imagine that this little pink pig has been fed and fattened. He grew up and one day they took him to the abattoir. The little pink pig had no idea what awaited him there. When he arrived he was knocked out with a club, then his throat was cut with a sharp knife. Then he was left to bleed out.

Then he was sliced into different cuts of meat: hams, filets, loin etc. These are the cuts you find on big white trays in supermarkets. The offal is used for ready meals or pet food. Eventually, only the skin and bones are left.

Then the skin and bones are placed in a huge pot. They're boiled for several hours until a foam forms on the surface: that's what we call pork gelatine.

And this gelatine is the main ingredient of the fizzy sweets you eat and offer to children. Sweets are made of the boiled skin and bones of little fattened pigs.

So now you know the true story of sweets.

The next time you fancy a sweet, remember this story.

Remember the little pink big, the blood running from his throat, his skin and bones boiling in a great pot...

Maybe you don't fancy it anymore? If that's enough, remember that to make the same sweets and give them a shiny look, sometimes a juice made of female ladybirds is used.

To give a taste of raspberry, crushed insects are used.

And secretions from the anal glands of the beaver, called "castoreum", enhance their flavour.

Bon appétit!

A study conducted by Lenoir et Al (2007) reached a surprising conclusion. In this experiment, the researcher had equipped a cage containing 2 rats with 2 levers:

- **Lever no. 1:** allowed the rats to dose themselves with cocaine intravenously,
- **Lever no. 2:** allowed the rates to have access, for 20 seconds, to sugar water.

In the first phase of the experiment, the rats only had access to the first lever enabling the distribution of cocaine. The second lever had been blocked. The rats started to become dependent on cocaine after the 9th day.

In the second phase of the experiment, the rats only had access to the second lever enabling the distribution of sugar water. The first lever had been blocked. They started to become dependent on sugar after the 7th day.

The researcher concluded that sugar created a dependency more quickly than cocaine.

In the third phase of the experiment, rats had access to two levers, the one distributing cocaine and the one distributing sugar water. They therefore had the choice between taking cocaine, drinking sugar water or doing both. In this phase of the experiment, 9 rats out of 10 preferred to consumer sugar rather than cocaine. Put another way, sugar is more addictive than cocaine. The researcher's conclusion was clear:

THE ADDICTIVE POTENTIAL OF SUGAR IS HIGHER THAN THAT OF COCAINE

The researcher continued his experiments. He showed that rats addicted to cocaine, even after a few weeks, were able to stop consuming cocaine if they were given the option of consuming sugar instead. The sugar was more attractive no matter how many doses of cocaine were taken.

All in all, the results of this study showed that 9 out of 10 rats prefer sugar over cocaine. This preference remains when doses of cocaine are increased, when rats are intoxicated with cocaine, when there is an escalation in the consumption of cocaine or they show a notable behavioural sensitivity to cocaine.

This study puts into context the effects of sugar on health and calls into question its introduction by makers into a huge range of food which normally lacks it. A ban on the use of glucose syrup has therefore been requested by a group of American researchers, particularly to protect the health of children.

Finally, you should be aware that as with drugs, the best way of protecting yourself from an addiction is never to start in the first place. Put another way, if you don't eat sugar, you don't run the risk of becoming addicted: so avoid fizzy drinks and fruit juices, and more generally all processed foods which are often full of sugar.

The 100 most sugar-rich foods:

1. Fructose
2. White sugar 99.00 g
3. Aspartame sweetener 98.70 g
4. Brown sugar 96.70 g
5. Meringue 91.80 g
6. Sweets 83.20 g
7. Chewing-gum 81.40 g
8. Sweetened chocolate powder 80.00 g
9. Honey 79.10 g
10. Fruit spread 71.10 g
11. Exotic dried fruit mix 68.10 g
12. Malted powder with added cocoa and sugar for drinking 65.40 g
13. Jelly sweets 64.50 g
14. Nougat 64.10 g
15. Strawberry jam 60.00 g
16. Biscuit free coated chocolate bar 59.40 g
17. Sweetened chocolate powder (or granules) 59.20 g
18. Raisins 59.20 g
19. Mint or raspberry syrup 58.90 g
20. Dried dates 58.10 g
21. Chocolate coated sweets 57.80 g
22. Chocolate and nut spread 57.60 g
23. White chocolate bar 57.10 g
24. Blueberry jam 57.10 g

25. Sweetened concentrated milk 55.90 g
26. Ladyfingers 55.00 g
27. Cherry jam 54.50 g
28. Almond paste 54.20 g
29. Jam (average portion) 53.90 g
30. Soft biscuits stuffed with orange
    and coated in icing 53.70 g
31. Chocolate coated peanuts 53.50 g
32. Apricot jam 53.40 g
33. Skimmed milk powder 51.80 g
34. Sponge cakes stuffed with fruit
    and coated with chocolate 51.20 g
35. Raspberry jam 50.80 g
36. A milk chocolate cereal bar 50.50 g
37. A bar of milk chocolate 50.50 g
38. Orange marmalade 49.20 g
39. Fruit cups 48.80 g
40. Vanilla chestnut cream (preserve) 48.70 g
41. Dried fig 48.10 g
42. Coconut bar coated in chocolate 48.00 g
43. Wafers stuffed with fruit 46.50 g
44. Chocolate bar with dried fruits 46.30 g
45. Gingerbread 44.90 g
46. A bar of milk chocolate with dried fruit 44.60 g
47. Powdered chocolate for babies 44.50 g
48. Cocoa pops enriched with vitamins
    and minerals 44.50 g
49. Soft macaroons stuffed with jam
    or cream 44.50 g
50. Dry biscuits stuffed with fruits 44.20 g
51. Semi-skimmed milk powder 43.90 g
52. Low sugar jam 43.60 g

53. Honey or caramel wheat grains enriched
with vitamins and minerals | 43 g
54. Cannelé | 42.50 g
55. Lemon tart | 40.90 g
56. Chocolate-coated biscuit bar | 40.60 g
57. Dried apricots | 40.50 g
58. A bar of dark chocolate with dried fruit | 40.50 g
59. A bar of dark chocolate
(minimum 40% of cocoa) | 40.40 g
60. Fruit cake | 40.10 g
61. Baklava | 39.60 g
62. Langues de chat | 39.50 g
63. Low fat fruit biscuits | 39.20 g
64. Wafer with or without chocolate | 38.70 g
65. Fondant chocolate cake | 38,50 g
66. Ground black pepper | 38.30 g
67. Chocolate Rocher | 38.20 g
68. Prunes | 37.90 g
69. Breakfast cereal bar, enriched in vitamins
and minerals | 37.70 g
70. Soft cake stuffed with chocolate or milk
or chocolate chips | 37.20 g
71. Biscuits stuffed with milk or vanilla | 37.20g
72. Sugared cornflakes enriched in vitamins
and minerals | 37.20g
73. Chocolate wheat flakes enriched
with vitamins and minerals | 37.00g
74. Whole milk powder | 36.20g
75. Dry biscuits coated in chocolate | 35.90 g
76. Crunchy dry biscuit (e.g.: tuile),
chocolate free, low-fat | 35.70 g
77. Chocolate brownie | 35.70 g

78. Baked Alaska   35.20 g
79. Chocolate layer sponge   35.00 g
80. Dry biscuits with chocolate   34.90 g
81. Cocoa pops enriched in vitamins
    and minerals   34.80 g
82. Chocolate cereal bar enriched with vitamins
    and minerals   34.70 g
83. Milk and chocolate biscuit   33.30 g
84. Raisin bread   33.20 g
85. Fruit cereal bar enriched with vitamins
    and minerals   33.10 g
86. Crisp bread stuffed with chocolate or fruit   33.00 g
87. Honey puffs enriched with vitamins
    and minerals   32.80 g
88. Baby cereals (6 months and above)   32.80 g
89. Dry biscuits stuffed with chocolate   32.50 g
90. Gazelle horns   32.00 g
91. Chocolate chip cookies   31.30 g
92. Dry biscuits stuffed with fruits   31.10 g
93. Uncoated chocolate cereals enriched
    with vitamins and minerals   31.00 g
94. Chocolate cereal bar   30.80 g
95. Dry chocolate packaged biscuits (pocket)   30.80 g
96. Dry biscuits and almond tuiles   30.80 g
97. Filled wafers (chocolate, vanilla, nuts etc.)   30.70 g
98. Chocolate cereals filled with chocolate
    or nuts and chocolate enriched with vitamins
    and minerals   30.10 g
99. Shortbread   30.10 g
100. Crunchy muesli with fruits   29.30 g

Data comes from the Ciqual 2012
nutritional table developed by the
French Agency for Food, Environmental
and Occupational Health Safety (ANSES).
Data is calculated for 100 grams of food.

So the prize goes to breakfast cereals, cakes and pastries, but also jam and dried fruits. All of these foods should be an exception in your diet, because they are high calorie foods. Above all the sugar they contain encourages sugar addiction and weight gain because simple carbohydrates, if they are not consumed, are immediately stored in the form of fat. Pay particular attention to the food given to children.

STAGE 8:
CHANGING YOUR HABITS

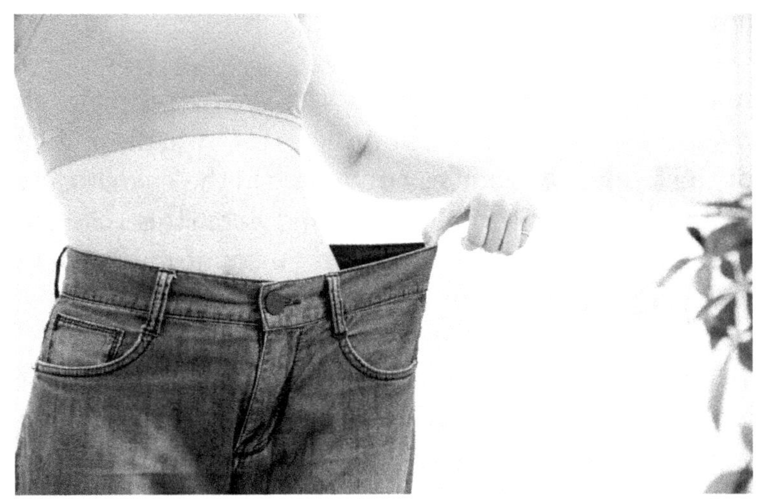

HABIT 1:
STOP WATCHING TV

I've always been a great fan of TV. When we were kids, my brother and I would spend entire Wednesdays sat in from of the *Club Dorothée,* a kids' show. When I was a teenager, I used to spend my evenings watching American TV movies. When I became an adult, my focus switched to news programs and political shows in addition to films and series.

And then one day I realised that the TV was taking up all my space. It held prime position like a totem in the middle of the lounge. As soon as I got home in the evening, my first reflex was to turn the TV on and watch the 8 o' clock news. I ate in front of the TV, then spent my evening watching films late into the night.

This behaviour, which I thought was harmless, was not without consequences for my health, particularly the way I ate. TV has a huge influence on the way we eat. Now we'll see why it's so vital to change your relationship with the TV if you want to lose weight.

① TELEVISION STOPS YOU EATING MINDFULLY

Television stops you eating mindfully. We are distracted by news, intrigued by a story, hooked by a film. We are absent, and while our brain is distracted, we eat too much and we eat poorly. As we are busy thinking about what's happening on the TV, we forget to think about what's happening on our plate and in our stomach. We ignore signals sent by our body such as feelings of fullness. Even if we've eaten too much, we don't feel full.

By eating in front of the TV, each time we risk eating more food than we need. We would definitely eat less if we were sat at the table and paying attention to what we feel. The same thing happens when you go to the cinema and buy popcorn or a bag of sweets. You eat without paying attention, engrossed in the film, consuming huge amounts of fatty and sugary foods without really noticing, even if you're not hungry.

② TELEVISION IS A STRESS FACTOR

If you step back for a moment, you realise that most television programs are stress-inducing. If you watch the news, almost every report depicts a world full of danger. Television causes negative emotions, broadcasting anxiety-producing scenes or stories. It's thanks to its ability to arouse positive emotions in us, but most often negative ones (such as anger, sadness or fear) that television is so popular.

The problem is that these negative emotions encourage the consumption of food. A stressed viewer needs to calm down. They use food as an anxiolytic. We saw earlier how food causes the secretion of "calming" hormones. Watching a stressful report or a terrifying scene in a film can cause stress levels to peak. This peak of stress levels can cause, in return, food cravings. People feel the need to eat because they need to calm down and know that food will help.

③ TELEVISION ENCOURAGES YOU TO EAT MORE

Pay attention to the contents of television adverts. You will notice that many of them sing the praises of certain foods, at specific times of the day. So I noticed that between 22h30 and 0h30, makers broadcast adverts for ice creams, biscuits or well-known cereals that are supposed to be eaten for breakfast. This is obviously done to encourage the consumption of foods at a time when people aren't normally eating. It's a way of increasing sales...

This is also why the last few years have seen an explosion of cooking programs on TV. It's not because cooking programs pull in good ratings, it's because behind these programs are big brands which can then place their food adverts in the breaks. You watch a cooking program. The adverts tell you what to buy. Television doesn't seek to make you happy or help you feel good or better; its role is purely business; that's all.

4 TELEVISION MAKES YOU MORE SEDENTARY.

The final point, and one of the most important, is that television makes you more sedentary. Rare are the viewers who watch their favourite shows while pedalling on an exercise bike. 99.9% of people sit on a comfortable sofa. The problem is that among that 99.9% of people, most of them have spent their day sat in front of a computer screen. If you work it out, some people only move a few minutes a day at most.

The aim of the big channels is not for you to live happy, healthy lives. They don't care at all. They're indifferent to your problems. They're there to do business, like the marketing men, the main brands of the agro-food industry and supermarkets. Their aim is to create programs that will attract your attention and keep you in front of your television for as long as possible. Their secret dream: a viewer who spends 24h a day in front of their TV.

Television: an obesity machine!

Television is an obesity machine. It's a device for shortening people's lives! Because the programs and adverts broadcast, and the behaviour it encourages are damaging to people's health. Generally we watch the TV because we don't know what else to do. We're bored, we feel alone, we need to think about something, something else. That's why we sit in front of the screen. It lets us escape, live intense experiences, adventures we'll never experience in real life.

Giving up TV means reinventing your life. It's a choice that requires imagination. But at the same time you're trading a life of TV and biscuits for a flourishing, enriching and stimulating life. I must admit that I'm only just starting to make progress in this area. I've made a promising start and I plan to continue. Getting out of the house, meeting people, living, loving, laughing and just you wait — you'll lose weight and live longer.

10 FUN ACTIVITIES TO HAVE FUN AND HELP YOU STOP WATCHING TV

① LEARNING TO PLAY A MUSICAL INSTRUMENT

Learning to play a music instrument is hugely satisfying, is a positive way of filling up your evenings and is a good way of entertaining friends and family. Hearing a friend or family measure play music is a huge pleasure.

② PLANT A VEGETABLE PATCH

Gardening has a scientifically proven anti-stress effect. Plants and fruit trees require daily care. By looking after them, you will reconnect with nature and in return get healthy, natural food for your plate.

③ SIGN UP TO AN IMPROV CLUB

And what about becoming the king of improve! It's a great way to stimulate your imagination, learn to improvise and express yourself in public. Taking and giving pleasure by entertaining an audience, what could be better?

4 GOING TO THE GYM

A cardio or body building session followed by a sauna or Turkish bath is the perfect way to relax after a stressful day at work. And many gyms also offer group activities for those who prefer them.

5 WALKING

There's nothing like a good walk in the fresh air to relax and unwind after dinner. Go for a walk and you'll see your sleep improve no end. You'll feel much better.

6 READ A BOOK

Reading is a sedentary activity. But at least it stimulates the imagination and the intellect, unlike television which is a purely passive activity. So read a book instead of watching the TV.

7 LEARN A FOREIGN LANGUAGE

Mastering a foreign language means opening the door to the world. It means creating opportunities to meet new people and discover new things. There are some excellent websites but also clubs and evening classes to practice conversation.

8 DO A MANUAL ACTIVITY

Knitting, sewing, painting, drawing, doing DIY…there are all the manual and creative activities you could desire. These manual activities are excellent ways of fighting stress and simply enjoying yourself.

9 GET ON A ROWING MACHINE, STEP MACHINE OR EXERCISE BIKE

There is a whole range of machines for doing sport without leaving the house. For people who prefer not to leave the house in the evening, or who are unable, these devices are a life saver. And that way you can watch a good film at the same time!

10 DO NOTHING

From time to time, just do nothing. I've tried, it's really hard! But I think it's something that can be learnt. Doing nothing, just being, watching the time past, is the most relaxing activity of all.

HABIT 2:
TREAT YOURSELF TO ORGANIC FRUITS AND VEGETABLES

Eating is a sensual activity. And this is where the agro-food industry is so successful. It's managed to invent products which flatter our tongue and encourage us to eat more and more. Eating fruits and vegetables can not only bring about the same type of gustatory please but also satisfaction that you'll ever got from consuming mass produced foods. Here are 3 ways in which eating organic fruit and vegetables is so satisfying.

1 THE SATISFACTION OF HELPING A PRODUCER MAKE A LIVING

Organic fruit and vegetables are grown on farms run on a human scale, by men and women who make a living from the vegetables they grow. Very often these are people who love their work and nature who have sacrificed their standard of living to produce quality foods. By consuming fruits and vegetables from short channels (organic baskets, fair trade, direct sale), you help these men and women make a living and get a decent return for their work.

Not only are you consuming fruits and vegetables that has been cared for, that has been grown with love, respecting biological balance, but you're also helping support the work of men and women who have a passion for their work. Whenever I eat fruits and vegetables from organic baskets I feel an immense satisfaction. What I do has meaning for me but also others. By eating, I'm doing a service for other men and women I don't even know. It's hugely gratifying.

② THE SATISFACTION OF TREATING YOUR BODY

Fruits and vegetables contain nutrients that are excellent for your health: vitamins, salts, minerals, antioxidants etc. Not only do fruit and vegetables taste delicious, but they also profoundly nourish the body and help it stay healthy. So added to the pleasure of taste is the pleasure of feeling that food is doing your body good. It cares for it like a drug. It gives it energy like a fuel. You're not just eating fruits and vegetables, but life itself!

Imagine broccoli gently steamed and sprinkled with a fine olive oil pressed by a smallholder from southern Spain. It's not just broccoli you're eating, it's Spain itself, the heat, the sunshine and the sea. Your body assimilates this broccoli and all its nutrients. It's like a gift. These nutrients protect you from cancer, eye problems, strokes. It's like an unguent that protects, repairs and cares for your body, battered by problems and cares.

③ THE SATISFACTION OF PROTECTING THE PLANET

By consuming fruits and vegetables from short channels, you're protecting the planet. You avoid thousands of tons of pesticides being sprayed on crops, pesticides that get into the air and water, which kill all the insects and poison other animals including human beings. Not only are you protecting your body but also the planet we live on, a planet with a fragile balance and suffering from the gradual disappearance of nature.

Eating fruits and vegetables creates a huge sense of satisfaction, in addition to doing your body good, by helping all the living beings on earth (plants and animals). So it's an action which makes sense for you and for others. It's both a selfish and altruistic act. Eating carrots might not be as good on the tongue as vanilla ice cream or chocolate éclairs, but the satisfaction you get from consuming it is so much better than between the two the choice is easy.

THE BENEFITS OF FRUIT

Here is a list of the best fruits for your health. Eating fruits is eating life! But remember, it's obviously best to eat organic fruit from short channels (organic baskets, direct sale, fair trade). You will feel 3 extra benefits compared with eating intensively farmed fruit bought from supermarkets.

1 APPLES

As an old English saying goes: "An apple a day keeps the doctor away". Indeed, apples have a host of health benefits. Firstly they reduce your appetite. The fibres and the pectin it contains make you feel full for longer. So it reduces the need to snack. It also reduces constipation and encourages good bowel transit.

2 MELONS

Melons are extremely rich in antioxidants, mainly carotenoids, which give them their orange colour. Melons are also very rich in beta-carotene, the precursor to vitamin A (which is essential for the growth and development of cells, vision and the immune system). They have 15 to 20 times more than yellow or green melons.

③ GRAPES

Grapes have antioxidant and anti-inflammatory properties, but their main benefit is that they protect the heart and the arteries, particularly in the event of excessive consumption of saturated fats. It's the famous "French Paradox" of people who live in the South West who eat a very fatty diet yet don't suffer from cardio-vascular illnesses.

④ ORANGES

Oranges are rich in vitamin C, stimulate the immune system and are a good way of fighting fatigue. A single orange covers almost all our daily needs. Vitamin C increases the absorption of iron, which is why it's particularly recommended for growing teenagers, women with heavy periods and mothers to be.

⑤ PINEAPPLES

Pineapples contain bromelin. This enzyme improves digestion. It thins the blood and reduces the risk of phlebitis. It also has anti-inflammatory properties, whence its use in the treatment of post-trauma and post-operative oedema, as well as tendinitis. Thanks to its anti-filtration power, it fights water retention and cellulitis.

⑥ APRICOTS

Apricots are veritable bundles of vitamin A, which is good for the health of the skin, eyes and immune system. Vitamin A is also great for iron metabolism. Apricots are therefore an excellent fruit for people with an iron deficiency.

⑦ CHERRIES

Cherries are a very important source of vitamin B9. They also contain folates. Folates help with the growth of maternal tissue during pregnancy, normal blood formation, psychological balance, the proper functioning of the immune system and the reduction of tiredness.

⑧ BLACKCURRANT

Blackcurrant, in addition to being extremely rich in vitamin C, contains potassium and manganese. Potassium contributes to the proper functioning of the nervous system and muscles, and maintaining normal blood pressure. Manganese helps protect the bones and protects cells against oxidant stress.

⑨ HAZELNUTS

Hazelnuts are an incredible source of nutrients, particularly at the beginning of winter, a period when the body is sorely tested by falling temperatures. Hazelnuts contain calcium, which is particularly good for strengthening the bones and teeth. So they are therefore recommended for children and the elderly.

⑩ NUTS

Suffice to say that it's hard to find a fruit richer in nutrients (copper, manganese, phosphorus, magnesium, iron, potassium and zinc). Zinc contributes to the normal synthesis of DNA, and fertility. These nutrients protect the bones, the hair, the nails and skin. They help you maintain normal testosterone levels in the blood.

The big cherry tree

I remember, when I was little, a big cherry tree. It stood in the midst of wheat fields in the very heart of Burgundy. I remember the blue sky of Burgundy, a dark blue sky, and the heat of June when I and the other kids from the village used to climb this cherry tree. It was covered with fruits, and we used to spend hours picking them from the tree. We used to amuse ourselves by hanging them from our ears like earrings, or spitting the stones as far as possible. Fearless, we would climb the highest branches, watching out for the farmer, who each year would rage "against the birds" who had eaten his lovely fruit.

I remember the endless pleasure of those afternoons. I'm sure you have similar memories. If you don't, I can heartily recommend such a unique experience. Eating a fruit picked directly from the tree is an extraordinary delight. It brings you closer to nature and the most ancient roots of human beings, as before being a farmer, man was a hunter-gatherer. Rediscover this pleasure as a change from supermarkets and a way to restore a bit of poetry, even spirituality, to food.

THE BENEFITS OF VEGETABLES

Vegetables, alongside fruits, are the natural foundation of the human diet. It's impossible to do without this inexhaustible source of mineral salts, vitamins and fibre. To such an extent that some people survive solely on fruit and vegetables. These foods are full of energy. Supplemented by cereals, they form the basis of a vegetarian diet. And there's no obesity problem among people who consume vegetables. These foods supply a lot of energy but few sugars and fats.

1 SOYA

This is one of the most interesting sources of vegetable proteins. Soya also contains phosphorus. Phosphorus contributes to a normal energetic metabolism, the proper functioning of cellular membranes, and helps protect the bones and teeth. Soya also contains folates, copper, vitamin B1 and manganese.

2 GREEN PEPPER

Pepper is rich in vitamin C and folates. But above all it contains vitamin B6. Vitamin B6 contributes to the normal functioning of the nervous system, the normal metabolism of proteins and glycogen, the formation of red blood, cells, the normal functioning of the immune system and regulation of hormonal activity.

③ CAULIFLOWER

Cauliflowers are rich in vitamin C. They contain folates and vitamin B9, but above all selenium. Selenium helps protect the hair and nails. It helps the thyroid function. It also encourages the formation of spermatozoa in men.

④ GARDEN PEAS

Garden peas contain vitamin A, folates, vitamin B9 and manganese, but above all copper. Copper is particularly good for a normal energetic metabolism, normal pigmentation of the hair, the normal transit of iron through the body, the normal pigmentation of skin and the normal functioning of the immune system.

⑤ SWEET POTATOES

They contain vitamin C, manganese and potassium, but above all vitamin B6. Vitamin B6 contributes to the formation of red blood cells, the proper functioning of the immune system, the reduction of fatigue and regulation of hormonal activity. Sweet potatoes are excellent metabolism regulators.

6 POTATOES

Potatoes contain numerous nutrients (Vitamin C, B6 and potassium), and particularly selenium. Selenium contributes to the maintenance of normal hair, nails and thyroid function, protects cells against oxidant stress, the normal functioning of the immune system and normal spermatogenesis.

7 PEARS

Pears contain folate and copper. Copper helps protect cells against oxidant stress, the normal functioning of the immune system, maintenance of normal conjunctive tissues, a healthy metabolism, the normal functioning of the immune system, the pigmentation of the skin and hair and the normal transit of iron through the body.

8 AVOCADOS

Avocados contain copper, folates, potassium, vitamin E, manganese, vitamin B6 and vitamin B5 or pantothenic acid. Pantothenic acid contributes to good energetic metabolism, better intellectual performance, the synthesis of steroid hormones, vitamin D and certain neuro-transmitters.

9 TOMATOES

They contain vitamin A and vitamin C. Vitamin A helps maintain normal skin, normal mucous glands, normal vision, the normal metabolism of iron and the normal functioning of the immune system. Tomatoes contain a lot of water and are very good for hydration.

10 GREEN BEANS

Green beans contain folates and selenium. Selenium contributes to the maintenance of normal hair, nails and thyroid function, protects cells against oxidant stress, the normal functioning of the immune system and normal spermatogenesis.

HABIT 3:
GET AN EXERCISE BIKE

The best way of taking up a physical activity is to have exercise equipment at home. I know all too many patients who've signed up to a gym, full of ambition and will, yet never set foot in it due to lack of time. Ideally, your gym should be at home, available and ready to go. In this way, come wind, rain or snow, you can exercise your body and get it moving.

Personally, I keep my exercise in my lounge. The TV's there, so why not my exercise bike? In this way, when I get home in the evening the first thing I see is that dear companion which has helped me, in just a few months, strengthen my thighs and buttocks and lose much of the extra fat I was carrying in that part of the body. It was my first step on the long journey to a more natural, active and less sedentary life.

Exercise bikes also have the advantage of being a gentle way of taking up a physical activity. They aren't traumatic. They don't require super human efforts. You can adjust the difficulty. In short, they have all sorts of advantages, and don't cost the earth. Today there are excellent foldable and ergonomic models (with a back rest), even having a certain style. Even in a study you can find room for an exercise bike which will give a certain style to your interior.

Ideally you should get a bike with a back rest to avoid backache and be able to read, play or watch conferences while you pedal. One of my close colleagues has even installed a desk on his exercise bike so he can work on his computer while pedalling. When it's time to do his accounts, he gets set up on his bike. He creates tables, does calculations and makes his forecasts. And when he finally raises his head he finds he's been pedalling for an hour and consumed 300 calories!

So do it! Grab your bank card. Go online. Type "Buy an exercise bike" in Google. And buy a model that suits you for between 100 and 200 Euros. That's enough. Wait patiently for it to arrive (I know you can't wait to try it), assemble it and then start pedalling for 15 to 20 minutes a day. Then gradually increase the time and the difficulty until you find it easier (and the desire) to do more, and open your mind to other sports.

Let's go!

HABIT 4:
STOP DRINKING ALCOHOL

ALCOHOL AND WEIGHT LOSS

A lot of people don't realise that alcohol makes you fat. Studies conducted on the subject have shown that not only is alcohol a highly calorific drink but its consumption encourages weight gain. Indeed, alcohol, by supplying large quantities of sugar, slows down the consumption of calories linked to food, particularly fatty and sugary foods, and therefore encourages the storage of these foods in the form of fat. Alcohol reduces the elimination of fat because the calories supplied by it are burnt very quickly, before those of fats.

Alcohol consumption therefore encourages the accumulation of fats. These fats are mainly stored in the abdomen, a common problem for big drinkers of beer, but also wine. Also, alcohol stimulates your appetite: put another way, the more you drink, the hungrier you get! Finally, alcohol reduces motor and attention skills. You have less self-control, which can cause food cravings for people on diets, or even bulimia crises. It is therefore highly recommended to avoid alcohol when trying to lose weight.

ALCOHOL AND HEALTH

In the same way as the consumption of certain foods is toxic, so is consumption of alcohol. Lobbyists, particularly from the wine industry, constantly highlight the beneficial effects of regular alcohol consumption. Yet independent studies have consistently failed to show any real beneficial effect from alcohol. Drink two glasses of red wine with lunch and see if your brain works as well as if you'd gone without. You merely run the risk of needing a siesta!

Between 15 and 25 I drank a lot of alcohol. I used to enjoy what young people modestly call "partying", which often consists merely of getting drunk. I still remember the monumental hangovers that were the result. The older I got the longer it took to recover, that is to say restore all my physical and intellectual faculties. And then one day I realised I was completely fooling myself. I had no need of alcohol to be happy.

As with food, before consuming alcohol you need to watch the whole film. And what's the whole film for alcohol? The whole film is that you drink and then, even with limited consumption, you get tipsy. You'll be more tired than usual and without your full capacities. You'll spend several unpleasant hours, even days, all for a few minutes of pleasure... Many people drink to fit in or out of habit. I recommend quitting and trying something else.

Of course, during a dinner, a cocktail or a family meal, you'll be offered alcohol. Learn to say "NO THANKS". There's no problem with saying "NO THANKS". Not drinking alcohol doesn't make you an ascetic! It just means you have another definition of what it means to have fun and be happy. You can be happy, have fun and laugh without drinking alcohol. There are hundreds of millions of people on this planet who never touch a drop. Try it and you'll see.

Table showing the equivalence between alcohol and calories:

(For information, a bar of chocolate represents around 500 calories).

- 1 glass of red wine at 10° (150 ml) = 82 kcal
- 1 glass of white wine at 11° (150 ml) = 105 kcal
- 1 glass of fortified wine, like Port (50 ml) = 80 kcal
- 1 glass of (150 ml) = 225 kcal
  (*Or about ½ a bar of chocolate / kir*)
- 1 glass of muscat (150 ml) = 240 kcal
- 1 vodka orange (150 ml) = 163 kcal

- 1 bloody Mary (150 ml) = 211 kcal
- 1 glass of champagne (150 ml) = 105 to 180 kcal (brut, dry)
- 1 beer (330 ml) = 125 to 200 kcal
- 1 glass of cider (150 ml) = 50 kcal
- 1 Martini (80 ml) = 128 kcal
- 1 glass of gin (80 ml) = 177 kcal
- 1 serving of pastis (40 ml) = 106 kcal
- 1 whisky (40 ml) = 100 kcal

A TRUE EPICURIAN!

Some people, when they see the changes you've made to your lifestyle, will say you have a boring life, that you've stopped making the most of life, that you're ascetic… Ignore them. These people are wrong! They think eating sugar and fat and drinking alcohol makes you happy. These people haven't understood the real way the body and mind operates. They're simply a step behind you in their personal development.

Because now you're an epicurean, a true epicurean finding pleasure in all aspects of life without moderation. When I talk of the pleasures of life, first of all I mean the pleasure you get from having a healthy body which produces happiness hormones, which generates well-being and energy, a body you're proud of and in which you feel comfortable, because it's light, flexible, energetic, high performing and able to take on any challenge.

You know that pleasure does not come from outside but from inside you. It's a form of wisdom that you've acquired by reading this book and applying its principles with commitment and discernment. You can be proud of what you've accomplished, and have the right to stand up for your new approach in the face of your loved ones, calmly and with peace of mind. If they want to ruin their health for the sake of superficial and ephemeral pleasures, that's their choice. You've simply made a different choice.

There's just one last hurdle before you're done with this program. And this is undoubtedly the hardest. It consists of embodying the new you. In any transformation, at one point the caterpillar needs to become a butterfly. That day it becomes a butterfly it must accept that it is a butterfly. I've known patients who've become butterflies and wanted to go back to being caterpillars. Being happy isn't as easy as it looks. Being happy is something you need to fully embrace!

STAGE 9:

EVOLVING TOWARDS
A NEW IDENTITY

EVOLVING TOWARDS
A NEW IDENTITY

I didn't recognise you!

One day Béatrice, one of my colleagues, told me this story.

She was walking down the street when she caught the eye of a young woman. She didn't know her. Yet she kept staring at her. As they approached each other, the young woman called her name. Béatrice stopped, surprised. She searched her memory for a few seconds in an attempt to give a name to the face. The situation started to become embarrassing. But she couldn't put a name to this stranger, and couldn't keep walking, not without being rude.

"Florence! the person eventually said. We did a teacher training course together a couple of years ago. Now do you remember? Her voice was cheerful but betrayed a certain fragility.

Béatrice remembered this course well, which had lasted several months. It was one of the reasons she had decided to switch to a teaching job. She remembered Florence well, someone she had developed a friendship with. She used to see her every day as part of the group of the same ten people during the course. They'd even prepared a joint dissertation. Béatrice remembered Florence but did not recognise the person standing in front of her in the street.

It was a very strange and unpleasant feeling.

In her memory, Florence was a very chubby person. She'd always dressed in baggy, bright-coloured clothes. She had full cheeks, full lips and small laughing eyes. Her hair was cropped short. She didn't wear makeup. She gave off a lot of energy and had a great sense of humour.

The young woman in front of her in the street was skinny and sleek. She was dressed in elegant clothes in subdued colours. She had long, wavy hair. She had big eyes and had taken care with her make up. She was giving off a completely different vibe. For Béatrice, she was a totally different person.

Finally Florence explained that she'd been on a diet and had lost almost 50 kg (110 lbs.). She did a lot of sport. Many things had changed in her life since the course. They chatted for a while before going their separate ways. Béatrice listened to everything she had to say, all the while having the impression of speaking to a stranger.

When Béatrice told me this story, she explained that even today she had the strange feeling that the person she'd met that day wasn't Florence. She knew that it was, but her brain refused to accept the idea, the two people were so different in every way.

The story of Florence and Béatrice is typical of what happens in cases of significant weight loss, but also in cases of minor weight loss. Because any weight loss, especially if accompanied by other physical transformations (hairstyle, make-up, perfume, clothes) constitutes a transformation of the person and therefore their identity.

This transformation (this evolution if you prefer) of the identity is particularly destabilising, both for the person's friends and family and for the person themself. It's a phenomenon very close to "depersonalisation". Imagine what Florence must have felt when Béatrice didn't recognise her.

Patients who have experienced this type of phenomena evoke a certain ambivalence. On the one hand they experience the satisfaction of seeing friends and family fail to recognise them, because it's irrefutable evidence of the fact that they've changed. On the other, they feel great anxiety at the feeling of no longer knowing who they really are.

One day a patient told me in this respect that he felt as if one night he'd gone to sleep and his brain had been transplanted into another body with a different face.

This phenomenon of "depersonalisation" is a major obstacle to weight loss because it can be an extremely complicated thing to experience and manage in psychological terms. Better understanding its mechanisms, causes and consequences will help you better manage this transition and avoid putting weight straight back on again and going back to your old habits.

Relationships with others are key to losing weight and changing your habits for good. This is why we are devoting an entire chapter to this question. And that's why, when losing weight, it's something you need to pay particular attention to. It's the secret of lasting weight loss!

Losing weight means changing your appearance. Yet appearance is one of the things that define a person's identity. Our loved ones, friends and work colleagues recognise the shape and expressions of our face, our silhouette, our stance, our attitudes and the way we move, but also our voice and smell. By losing weight, particularly when you lose a lot, you change many of these things. The things that make us stand out and define our identity are therefore changed.

A change in appearance is very often amplified by the people themselves. It's common for a person who's lost weight to take the opportunity to change their hairstyle, make up or perfume. They'll also be tempted to completely change their wardrobe and the way they dress. This massively amplifies the physical transformation alone. This was the case with Florence, who in addition to losing 50 kg, had grown her hair and drastically changed the way she dressed.

The way people behave and, to a certain extent, their values, are also changed. Someone who stops eating the same food (for example she had given up cakes) will stop going to the same places (for example she had stopped going, or went less frequently, to her favourite tea shop), which can change their relationships with friends and family (she used to go to the tea shop twice a week with her best friend, who she now saw a lot less). Tastes, values, aspirations, habits and relationships change.

Our friends and family have often known us for many years. They recognise us through what they know of us: our desires, our wishes, our habits. By adopting new habits to lose weight and live better, we change these markers. These changes create a divergence between what is expected of us and the way we actually behave. We are different. These changes can surprise people or win them over, but also, in many cases, annoy them, disturb them, bore them.

Also, changes to our tastes and behaviour mean we would like our friends and family to share our way of thinking. Think about someone who's started doing a lot of exercise to lose weight. Not only has this activity helped them lose weight, but they will have discovered and experienced the benefits for their health. Surely it's natural for them to want to share this discovery with their loved ones? Surely it's natural for them to want their friend and family to take up exercise as well?

All humans, to be happy, need to share their tastes, aspirations, values and habits. Sharing is essential to happiness. But when our tastes, aspirations, values and habits change, we need to recognise something: what we share with our loved ones is reduced. If they aren't evolving in the same direction, then naturally you'll "distance" yourself from them, as surely as in geometry two lines that are not parallel move apart as they approach infinity.

This "distancing" can be extremely painful. You have the feeling of no longer being able to share the essential things in life with the people you love. You love them, you'd like to continue sharing things with them, but this possibility is reduced. So you're on the horns of a dilemma:

- **Either you give up change:** you keep the same habits and same life style so you can continue sharing the essential things in life with the people you love. This is the choice made by people who'll go on to rapidly regain their weight.

- **Or you try and convince them to change as well:** this requires considerable energy and runs the risk of being unsuccessful. It can be hard on people who don't want to change.

- **Or you accept the "distancing"** and the suffering that results: in this case you'll need to change your relations with your friends and family and create new relationships with other people so you can start sharing again, something which is essential for our existence.

When you set out to lose weight and make a lasting change to your lifestyle, you will all face, at a given moment, this pivotal choice. It's a choice which isn't easy to make. But it has to be made, because otherwise the process will fail, and the changes you want won't last. People who go on yoyo diets are as much victims of their physiology (the body's tendency to fight against deprivation by storing fats) as their sociology (the tendency to refuse to change for fear of "distancing" themself from their friends and family).

Going on a diet means temporarily changing your habits, only to return to them afterwards. For example someone who goes out regularly for drinks with their friends might stop drinking while on a diet. For their friends, they're still the same person: someone who likes a drink but is abstaining. Their relationships won't change because they continue to share the same habits, the same values and the same tastes. It's just that one of them has been forced to temporarily give up this habit.

Now, if this person completely gives up drinking because they feel alcohol is bad for their health, they become a different person. They no longer have the same habits, the same values or the same tastes as their friends and family. Yet their relationship was partly based on the fact of sharing these habits, values and tastes. Part of the foundation of their relationship has therefore gone.

And if going out for drinks was the only time they saw each other, I'd be willing t0 be they see each other less often or even not at all.

My brother

My brother is what you'd call a "bon viveur". He loves wine and good food. With my cousins and his friends, it's common to spend a whole evening drinking and eating.

Until I was 25, I admit I used to share this same desire to "party". Once I reached 25 I started to pay more attention to my health. I started to become less and less interested in these evenings. The older I got, the less I enjoyed such evenings, because I felt I was poisoning my body. I wanted to be in shape and feel good.

A divide started to form between my brother and me, because he still enjoyed these evenings.

He still invited me round, but the more time went by, the earlier I'd leave. Soon I started finding excuses not to go. Excuses he didn't find particularly acceptable.

On the one hand I was unable to tell him that I no longer enjoyed that type of evening, and on the other I no longer felt like going because once there I felt obliged, to fully participate in the festivities, to drink and eat like everyone else. If you're in a group, then you're supposed to share things! But if I was honest, I felt uncomfortable during the evening, needing to control myself. The next morning, without fail, I would regret going.

As I wanted to live in a way consistent with my values and aspirations, I ended up no longer going to these evenings. And he also stopped inviting me. But this was the same not only for these evenings but also for birthday meals of my nephews or sister in law. Because when my brother organises a meal, it's always a huge "Blow out". We're at the table from 12h to 18h! This is the tradition in our region and in our family.

For my brother, these are big days. They're celebrations. He loves cooking, eating and drinking wine. While for me, these were boring days. Even before I ate I was already thinking of the stomach ache I'll end up with. Which is terrible, because I had the choice between going and feeling bad, or not going and being rude. In the end I decided to stop going. I'd rather be rude if it meant staying true to my beliefs. I'm sure he found me impolite and disrespectful. On the other hand, I was finding it harder and harder to understand the way he lived. I couldn't understand why he was sticking to his toxic behaviour. He's 40 now, and it pains me to see how he continues to mistreat his body. I think that over time we've developed completely different values, habits and beliefs.

I've tried to suggest other activities together: going mountain biking, going out for a coffee or taking the kids to a theme park at the weekends. He's always said no. He's always been busy. Maybe he wasn't interested, or maybe he didn't want to make the effort because he didn't think I was. Gradually we've started to see each other less and less. Now we only see each other once a month for lunch at my parents.

I'm telling you this story to show you the extent to which the lifestyle changes necessary to lose weight can cause you to become distanced from certain friends and family. But you also need to see the positives. These changes can also bring you closer to other people. It's the perfect opportunity to make new friends, to get back in touch with other family members. If I talk of distancing, it's because it can be a source of suffering, and sometimes this is an obstacle to maintaining good habits in the long term.

But there is also reconciliation. By losing weight, not only did I restore my health, well-being and joie de vivre but also met loads of people I had never met before. I was open to new activities and met new people who have now become almost like friends. Distancing yourself from certain people also means getting closer to others. Don't worry. Just accept that your relationships with others will change.

5 TIPS TO ACHIEVE CHANGE

① STAND UP FOR YOURSELF

You have the right to change. You have the right to have values, behaviours and habits that are different from your friends and family. You have the right to have a different approach to life and different pleasures to your friends and family. You just need to stand up for yourself. The best way of achieving change is to see this change as something irreversible. Your friends and family should sense no weakness in your determination to change. If they perceive your change as irreversible they'll be forced to adapt.

② EXPLAIN YOUR CHOICES

Standing up for yourself doesn't mean imposing your views. You should also explain: explain why you've changed your habits by doing more exercise, explaining why you've stopped drinking alcohol all the time, explaining why you're eating less even during special meals. Explaining will give meaning to your acts and avoid misinterpretation. Your step mother will understand you not going back for thirds of her delicious chocolate cake, which is also a calorie time bomb!

❸ RESPECT OTHER PEOPLE'S CHOICES

The first reaction may be to try and "convert" your friends and family to your new life style. It's true that it's much easier to keep a lifestyle up if you share it with the people you love. This desire to share may be misinterpreted by friends and family, who feel you're lecturing, or trying to change their habits. Don't do it! Actions speak much louder than words. It's be reinforcing the positive changes in your life that others will want to make the same changes.

❹ FIND A GROUP OF LIKE MINDED PEERS

Among the people you know, some of them may have already adopted a healthier lifestyle. Use this opportunity to get closer to them. If not, join social media forums to meet people who have the same interests and desires as you. This will help you feel less alone. It will give you the strength to maintain your new behaviour and habits in the long term.

❺ COME UP WITH NEW WAYS OF GETTING TOGETHER WITH FRIENDS AND FAMILY

Maybe you only see your friends and family for drinks, lunch or dinner, and would like to see them in different settings. It's up to you to come up with new ways, and new settings, for sharing time with them. There are hundreds of activities you can enjoy together. They might be sceptical at first, but they'll enjoy themselves so much they'll end up wanting to do it again. It's up to you to take the lead! And if they're not interested, then that's their loss!

8 ACTIVITIES YOU CAN DO WITH YOUR FAMILY OR FRIENDS

① ORGANISE A WALK IN THE FOREST

From 7 to 77, everyone can go walking. Suggest a long walk in the forest with your friends or family. Breathe, discover plants, observe the animals, young and old will find something to enjoy.

② GO TO THE CINEMA OR THE THEATRE

There's nothing like going to the cinema or theatre for creating happy memories together. You could also go and see a comedian, a sure fire way of spending an unforgettable evening laughing and having fun.

③ GO SWIMMING

What could be nicer, after doing a few lengths, than chilling out in the Jacuzzi and chatting with your friends? You're treating your body and taking the opportunity to chat and spend time with people you like.

④ GO FOR A JOG

A jog is a perfect opportunity to talk and exchange ideas. The tongue is loosened as the body runs. You talk, you tell stories, you learn things from each other. You spend time together.

⑤ GO CANOING

Every town in France is close to a river, and somewhere to hire canoes. Hire canoes for the day and row down the river. In the evening, your head full of sensations, you'll sleep like a log.

⑥ GO TO A THEME PARK

Perfect for people with kids, a trip to a theme park is a chance for young and old to create unforgettable memories. They come in many different sizes, and some cost more than others, but you're really assured of a great time.

⑦ GO FISHING

If you're patient and love nature, fishing is for you. It's free, or almost. You'll spend the whole day in the sunshine, waiting for the fish to bite. No matter what you catch, you'll have a great time.

Introduce your friends or family to the pleasures of knitting, painting or sketching. It will keep your hands busy while you chat, discuss things in common or the world at large.

HOW DOES IDENTITY ACTUALLY WORK?

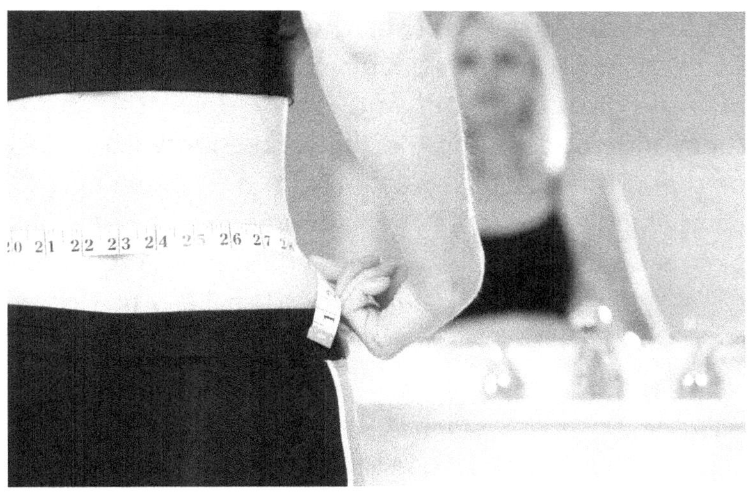

To properly understand the impact of changes due to weight loss on your life and relationships with others, first you need to understand how identity is constructed.

IDENTITY IS CONSTRUCTED THROUGH A "PERMANENT DIALOGUE" BETWEEN WHAT WE FEEL INSIDE AND OTHER PEOPLE'S PERCEPTION OF US.

Other people are like a mirror. Through our relationships with them (what they say about us, their criticisms, their compliments, their comments, their observations, we constantly define who we are. We adapt our behaviour and thinking according to this "reflection" to maintain a stable identity. If any human being aspires to change, they aspire, at least as much, to a form of continuity. Put another way, we want to have and give a stable image of ourselves.

For example, a person sees themselves as generous. As this is how they see themself, they act generously, offering gifts to friends and family, doing things for them and not counting the time and energy expended on them. Their friends and family, by their comments or compliments, reinforce their self-image as a generous person. So their identity is confirmed. Whenever someone says they're generous, they feel external affirmation of their self-view.

THE IMAGE THEY SEE IN THE "MIRROR" OF OTHERS IS CONSISTENT WITH THEIR OWN SELF-IMAGE.

Now let's imagine that her friends and family convey a different image. For example they show themselves to be indifferent to her acts of generosity. Imagine they stop telling her she's a generous person and even tell her she's stingy. Here, a divergence is created between her own self-image and what others tell her. This divergence will become a source of great anxiety. She doesn't know who she is anymore. And if she doesn't know who she is, she no longer knows how to behave.

IT'S LIKE GETTING UP ONE MORNING AND NOT RECOGNISING YOURSELF IN THE MIRROR! IT'S TERRIFYING!

The crisis of adolescence

In the West, we often refer to the age between 12 and 18 as a crisis of adolescence, characterised by different phenomena such as rebellion against adults, risky behaviour, depression etc. Adolescents have a reputation for being "uncomfortable in their skin". Psychology can explain why, at this precise period, adolescents present such symptoms. Understanding this will help us better understand what happens during weight loss.

When someone is a child, they're perceived by adults as a child. The role of a child is to play, go to school and be educated by adults. Also, children need protection, love and teaching to grow. Children completely understand their roles, rights and duties. What they feel is consistent with how adults act around them. This consistency means they are psychologically stable and enjoy harmonious relationships with friends and family.

With puberty, children's bodies change. They get taller and chubbier, while secondary sexual characteristics appear (hips and chest for girls, facial hair and a broken voice for boys). Our expectations of them change rapidly. Adults expect them to be more independent in their day to day life but also at an affective level. They want to be able to trust them. They also afford them less affection and protection. Children have to develop their own affective life.

Yet children don't immediately realise that their body's changing. They live in a child's body, behave like a child and still think like a child. They expect adults to treat them like a child. The problem is that adults' attitude to them changes, because with their physical changes they've stopped seeing them as children. They see them as adolescents, that is to say an adult in the making. So a divergence is created between their own self-image and how others see them.

This divergence is a source of great anxiety. Indeed, a young adolescent doesn't know precisely what is expected of them. They don't know because they have no idea what it means to be an adolescent, let alone an adult. Nobody's explained it. Also, adults can sometimes have an ambiguous attitude to them. They're no longer children, but they're not quite adults. This isn't clear to their parents or teachers. For example, they might still be chubby-faced like a child but have a deep voice like an adult.

This ambiguity is carried over into the rights and duties expected of them. For example, the parents of an adolescent ask him to make big decisions about their education because they want him to become an adult and take responsibility for his life. At the same time they stop him going out on Saturday night with his friends or going to bed late on the pretext that he's still too young. On the one hand they want him to be an adult, be responsible and independent, and on the other he's stuck in his role as a child.

Adolescence is not therefore a crisis of personality but a crisis of relationship between the child and adults. And this crisis isn't the fault of the child or the adult but both. Now we will see how what happens during adolescent crises is similar, although for different reasons, to what happens during weight loss and a change in behaviour to achieve this weight loss. Understanding this is crucial to ensuring that weight loss is sustainable.

Overweight people are perceived as being "curvy". Yet society (as we will see in greater detail in this chapter) attributes a certain number of roles and qualities to "curvy" people. When this person becomes "skinny", they are no longer perceived in the same way by their friends and family. The roles expected of them and the qualities attributed to them are no longer the same. So there is a divergence between the way people see themselves and other people's perception of them.

And this divergence can cause, as in adolescent crises, great anxiety.

They no longer feel recognised by their friends and family. They're seen differently. Also, the behavioural changes that have enabled this weight loss are not necessarily accepted by their friends and family. For example, a woman who always used to cook nice tasty dishes (i.e. fatty and sugary dishes) and starts cooking only healthy dishes based on fruits and vegetables might not be looked kindly on by her family members. So this creates tensions between the person and their friends and family.

Someone who eats fruit and vegetables, does sport and doesn't drink will not be perceived in the same way, or be attributed the same qualities, as someone who likes drinking a "good wine" or a "nice piece of steak". I put quotation marks around the expression "good" because you rarely hear about a person eating "good fruit" or "good water". "Good" is the adjective which marks out the common experience of pleasure. There is the "bon vivant" and the ascetic, and these two people do not have the same value.

It's not only hunger, a lack of discipline or physiology that makes people who've lost a lot of weight put it all back on again so quickly, but a range of psychological and social factors that then affect their physiology. Because anxiety, as we've seen above, plays an important role in regulating appetite. People often put weight back on again to restore their lost identity and reduce tensions with their friends and family.

Lasting weight loss means you need to change your identity and relationships with your friends and family.

Someone who loses weight, especially if they lose 10 kg or more and profoundly change their lifestyle, must accept becoming a different person, perceived differently by their friends and family and having different types of relationships with them. They have to accept a period of internal crisis necessary for the evolution of this new identity, and possible tensions with their friends and family. They need to accept, as we will see, breakups. Losing weight, as I know all too well, can often lead to separation.

THE "BON VIVANTS" – SUPER HEROES?

In the collective imagination, the "bon vivant" is an extraordinary figure. The capacity to drink wine and make merry is in itself special, such that "bons vivants" are somewhat admired. We admire their capacity to eat and drink in the same way we admire intelligence or strength in others. "Bons vivants" are in some way the elite sportsmen of food. The meals they eat are seen as exploits. They attract attention and attraction for this reason.

In groups of adolescents, we also find this type of challenge. On evenings out, adolescents compete in their capacity to eat and/or drink. Online you can find hundreds of videos of such competitions organised informally among groups of friends, or indeed officially. These "competitions" have existed since the dawn of time, and their winners become true legends. Once again, "bons vivants" are extraordinary people.

In literature we can find no end of such attractive personalities with statuesque bodies possessing this extraordinary capacity to eat impossible amounts of food and drink. Obélix is the perfect example. These are characters from ancient tales of giants and generally boast impressive physical strength. But their superiority comes above all from their appetite. So Obélix is capable of eating several wild boars in a single meal. And we find this amusing, impressive, sweet.

You should never under-estimate the influence of the collective sub-conscious on our behaviour. I think that many "bon vivants" eat and drink so much because it's a way of standing out from others. Eating becomes a way of existing and standing out from the herd. Because they eat more than everyone else, it means they're not like others. They're like Obélix, extraordinary beings, because they're able to exceed the normal limits of a human body.

That's why they have a certain charisma. We attribute special powers to them. They stand out from the crowd. Charismatic people are inherently different from others because of certain aspects of their appearance. Charisma is prized by many because of its seductive and attractive powers which are a boon for your career, business and love life etc. So there are real benefits to being a "bon vivant" and standing out.

The day these people lose weight, normally for health reasons, they find themselves forced to give up all these benefits. They have to give up what differentiates them from others, what makes them unique and charismatic people, and all the privileges this brings. They have to become ordinary people, subject like everyone else to the contingencies and limits of the physical body. And it's really hard to give up such an identity. It's almost impossible even.

That's why some people prefer to die from over eating and drinking rather than lose weight. Actual death sometimes pales into insignificance compared with the "social death" of losing what distinguishes you from others. For these people, slimming means becoming an ordinary person. And becoming an ordinary person means disappearing. These people are often very ambitious people, who want to shine and be recognised by as many people as possible, for their talents and abilities.

To get these people to lose weight, they have to become extraordinary in a different way. They can of course develop another talent in the field of work, arts or human relationships. They can of course develop a different physical capacity that is more compatible with their health. Even before starting to lose weight, they need to find something to replace their corpulence and be recognised and admired.

Here are a few examples of ways to shine without eating and drinking:

- Having a successful professional career,
- Being well travelled,
- Getting tattoos,
- Dressing unusually, always in fashion or extravagantly,
- Excelling in a sport, a game or creative activity,
- Being able to play a musical instrument,
- Being able to speak one or several foreign languages,
- Having a good sense of humour and the ability to make people laugh,
- Being a video game champion,
- Being an expert in IT and the Internet,
- Being a great mother or father,
- Being able to cook delicious healthy meals.

It doesn't matter what you choose, but you must choose something that differentiates you from others. It used to be your weight, your size, your appetite that made you stand out. Now it's something else. It's up to you to discover how you wish to grow. Especially if you need to flourish, stand out, exist.

CHANGING YOUR WEIGHT MEANS CHANGING YOUR CHARACTER!

Who could believe that?

Neither would I if I weren't a specialist in psychology. But it's the exact truth!

By changing your diet, by losing your excess weight, will you change your character?

How is that possible?

Quite simply because your friends and family will change their perception of you.

How do your friends and families influence your character?

You might think that your character is something immutable, inherent to you, unchangeable, except for becoming stronger and more asserted.

Nothing could be further from the truth.

Our character can change radically if the people around us attribute a different one to us. This is the principle of the Pygmalion effect.

I've seen it on several occasions in several fields. I've seen people change their character radically right after moving abroad or changing their job. By changing their reference groups, they had changed the way others saw them. And that was enough to profoundly change their character.

I'm sure you know people who've undergone a radical personality change after getting divorced and remarrying…It's the same phenomenon.

How does this change take place?

"Curvy" people are attributed certain qualities and faults by society, while "skinny" people are attributed other qualities and faults. These qualities and faults are nothing more than generalities, stereotypes.

Stereotypes have a great influence on people, because often they're internalised. "Curvy" and "skinny" people internalise the stereotypes that society has constructed for them.

They conform to them, if you prefer.

A "shy" little 4-year-old girl

My daughter is 4. One day I went to a parent-teacher meeting. We were to discuss what she had learnt and the progress made at nursery (bravo to the French school system which puts pressure on our little ones from the age of 3).

As we chatted, her teacher said: your daughter <u>IS</u> shy. She has problems expressing herself in a group setting. As she said these words, I saw my daughter, who had come with me, paying close attention. Your daughter IS shy, she repeated.

The teacher had observed her a dozen times in group sessions. She'd seen her blush and hide behind her hands when it came to reading a poem out loud, and she'd deduced one stable and lasting character trait from this: shyness.

Now my daughter had a label. Her character traits were starting to define her. Under the gaze of this adult who already had a great influence over her, she was sub-consciously starting to reflect her views.

By reasoning in this way, this schoolteacher had failed to realise that she'd effectively made my daughter shy because she was conforming to the label she'd been given. Instead of changing for the better (which is what her teacher sincerely wanted, as she was a kind person full of good intentions), my daughter was, on the contrary, trying to avoid speaking in public by hiding behind the label she'd been stuck with. This label was a kind of defence. Why make the effort to speak in public, to take this risk and be uncomfortable if I <u>AM</u> shy. After all, that's what I'm like. There's nothing I can do about it.

How many parents, teachers and educators make this mistake of attributing a personality trait to a child?

You must have heard such phrases when you were little:

- *He's a bit slow.*
- *He's such a chatterbox!*
- *He's brave and hardworking!*
- *He's a very wise child!*
- *He's so unruly!*

We generalise behaviour. In so doing, we drive children to reproduce this behaviour. When the adjectives are positive, it's a smart way of stabilising positive behaviour and making it last. But when they are negatives, we instil character traits in children that have a profound impact on their self-estimation.

The mechanism is the same for a "curvy" person. If everyone who sees a man with a big stomach and round cheeks says: "There's a bon vivant", there's a strong chance that he'll end up conforming to what people say about him. He'll continue to eat and drink all the more to continue being perceived as a "bon vivant".

You should be aware that this has a formidable influence. Often it operates without our knowledge, via the sub-conscious. And resisting it requires a lot of energy and willpower. Of course it's possible. Not every "curvy" person is a "bon vivant". This means you must at least be aware of the stereotypes that others associate with us.

The first thing I did after this meeting with her teacher was to have a talk with my daughter. I said more or less this:

"Darling, know that you're not shy. It's just that sometimes you don't feel like talking in front of the group; sometimes it's just not the right moment for you. You'll have plenty of other chances to do it. I'm sure you have the ability to talk in front of a lot of people. I'll help you do it. You'll gain self-confidence and then it'll be as easy as watching a cartoon."

In doing this, I ripped off the label…at least I hope so.

Human psychology functions in such a way that we tend to conform to stereotypes. This process of internalisation causes us to integrate certain qualities and certain faults that we wouldn't have spontaneously developed.

Now we'll look at the qualifiers attributed, in general, to "curvy" and "skinny" people. The following table was drawn up on the basis of different surveys carried out on social media as I wrote this book.

The data is indicative and not exhaustive.

TABLE OF ADJECTIVES USED TO DESCRIBE "SKINNY" AND "CURVY" PEOPLE

This table was created on the basis of different surveys conducted in March 2016 on social media, which 205 people aged between 15 and 59 participated in. The table should be read according to the logic of extremes. Thus, the "skinnier" a person is, the more "serious" they are perceived as being. Conversely, the "curvier" someone is, the more "relaxed" they are perceived as being. The adjectives in the left column are associated with "skinny" people and the adjectives in the right hand column are associated with "curvy" people.

THIN SKINNY	CURVY OBESE
Serious	Relaxed
Ascetic	A bon vivant
Boring	Happy
Upstanding	Clumsy
Cold	Warm
Rational	Emotional
Hard	Soft
Stingy	Generous
Strong willed	Weak willed
Perseverant	A quitter
Charming	Sensual
A manipulator	Easily manipulated
Frigid	Loves sex
Sterile	Fertile
Fragile	Protective
Masculine	Maternal

The terms given show how stereotypes differentiate between "skinny" and "curvy" people when it comes to a range of qualities and faults. Beware, these are stereotypes. Stereotypes tell us nothing about what these people are really like, their aspirations or what they'd like to be. They are just categories in which people pigeon hole us to get a quick idea of what we're like, anticipate our reactions and behaviour and adapt their own behaviour in return.

THE STEREOTYPE OF "SKINNY" PEOPLE

"Skinny" people are perceived as people who have a good level of control over their life. They have better control over their behaviour, their emotions and their feelings. This better control creates the impression that they are dominant in their inter-personal relations. Put another way, they know what they want and are capable of implementing the strategies necessary to get it. So we imagine them to be more calculating, more strategic, but also more interested and therefore more rational.

On the other hand, they're perceived as having few feelings and emotions. So they appear to be less warm, colder and harder in their inter-personal relationships. The feel less focused on others than "curvy" people. They appear less spontaneous. They also have the reputation of have less of a sense of humour and finding it more difficult to relax. It's the flip side of the coin. So they're less reassuring in their inter-personal relationships than "curvy" people, who immediately attract sympathy.

THE STEREOTYPE OF "CURVY" PEOPLE

The terms given show that "curvy" people are perceived as being dominated in inter-personal relations. They seem easier to manipulate than "skinny" people. They seem more emotional, leading one to think that they are also more sincere, because they are less able to hide their feelings. Again, these are stereotypes, but these stereotypes have a great impact because they explain why people are more attracted to "curvy" people than "skinny" ones.

"Curvy" people have a maternal image which has an ancient pedigree in our civilisation. The loving, protective and nourishing mother, against the hard and aggressive father, lacking feelings. This is the play between "curviness" and "thinness", it's the opposition between feminine values on the one hand and masculine values on the other, with all that is attached to these values. Further in this chapter we'll see that these values are not without consequence on the life of people who go from fat to thin, and vice versa.

SOCIAL ADVANTAGES AND DISADVANTAGES LINKED TO BEING CURVY AND SKINNY

The following text might shock people who seek an ideal of social justice. These people generally aspire to live in a society where there is strict equality of opportunity between people, regardless of their geographical or ethnic origin, and whatever their appearance. I share this ideal, but I've noticed, over the course of different discussions, that these people find it hard to accept the fact that social justice does not exist, and that human societies do not operate on these principles.

The work of Amadieu (2005), which collected hundreds of scientific studies on the role of appearance in education, professional and social success, showed that appearance plays a central role in a person's chance of success. Put another way, appearance often prevails over competence, hard work or effort. Being "skinny" or "curvy" changes our appearance and therefore changes our life chances, because it changes the way others perceive us.

I have analysed the advantages and disadvantages of being a "skinny" and a "curvy" person in today's society. It's vital to be aware of these advantages and disadvantages.

Why? Because if you're a "curvy" person and become "skinny", you'll automatically inherit the advantages and disadvantages of being a "skinny" person. Beware, what is an advantage for some might be a real disadvantage for others.

Everything written here corresponds to stereotypes forced on people and not reality.

① THE ADVANTAGES OF BEING A "SKINNY" OR "CURVY" PERSON

"Skinny" people are generally perceived as dominant. They give the impression of making fewer mistakes. They are therefore more credible at a professional level than people who are overweight. This generally allows them to advance more easily in their career. "Skinny" children, for their part, receive better reports from their teachers. Being "skinny" favours access to positions of responsibility, more regular salary raises and means a more interesting career.

It's clear that if you want to have a career, get a promotion or improve your grades, you should immediately lose weight. It's almost a condition *sine qua non*. I realise how shocking what I write might be. Yet it's merely the truth. I ask anyone who doubts what I say to look at certain scientific studies collected in Amadieu's key work (2005), called Le poids des apparences (the weight of appearance). Those of a sensitive disposition should look away…

For "curvy" people, being overweight gives them an advantage in inter-personal relations. It's easier for them to make new friends, to meet new people. As they appear nicer, we are more easily attracted to them. This personality trait we attribute to them can be an important advantage in activities with a large social component. Being overweight can help them excel in sales, politics or working with children.

② THE DISADVANTAGES OF BEING "SKINNY" OR "CURVY"

We are less forgiving of a "skinny" person than a "curvy" person. We are less attracted to them because we see them as colder. "Skinny" people are perceived as being more aggressive, more competitive and therefore more dangerous than "curvy" people, who we find it easier to see as protective and empathetic. This means that being "skinny" requires greater efforts to make friends and forge relationships with others.

For a "curvy" person, the problem is that when they reach a certain level of authority, people generally tend to trust them less. We doubt their capacity to make the effort, to go the extra mile, to demonstrate perseverance. So we're reluctant to entrust them with important tasks or offer them positions of responsibility. Being chubby is a brake on career advancement, particularly for women who are already at a disadvantage. We trust "curvy" people less when it comes to technical activities.

It's highly probably that a "curvy" person who becomes "skinny" will see a change in their relationships with friends and family.

It's highly probable that in professional terms they are given fewer responsibilities and people listen less to what they have to say.

This can be an opportunity but also a source of a certain amount of anxiety.

A "curvy" person is protected by their size, protected because they are forgiven more easily, less is expected of them, people are less demanding with them. So it can be tempting to put weight back on to avoid exposing yourself.

Not being taken too seriously can sometimes be an advantage in day to day life.

A "curvy" person who becomes "skinny" also has every chance of finding interpersonal relationships much harder than they used to.

Before, people would turn to them spontaneously. Their chubby faces reassured them. But now that their look is more chiselled, harder, people are more reluctant.

Suddenly, the "curvy" person can have the impression of being more isolated, harder to forge relationships.

I remember in the past I used to know "curvy" people who didn't have a particularly good sense of humour, but who we found funny just because of their weight. Indeed, some comedians play on their physiognomy. I remember seeing Coluche when I was a kid and wanting to laugh. He knew how to make the most of his corpulence to make people like him from the start.

Change can therefore be very destabilising because suddenly, the "curvy" person needs to learn to rely on different aspects:

- How to say NO when they're entrusted with responsibilities they never even used to consider?

- How to approach others when they used to be approached spontaneously?

- How to accept that others are now more demanding? That they are less forgiving?

Someone who loses weight might feel that their life has become more difficult. Before, being overweight created physical problems that they had learnt to manage. Now that they've lost weight, there are new challenges to face.

That's why so many people lose the weight they've lost: because they can't adjust to this new life, because they don't give themself time to learn how to adapt.

A female politician

I once advised a female politician who wanted to lose weight. In the political arena, contact with electors is key to success. Being able to "shake hands", make people like you, bring people together, but also avoiding enmity are all necessary skills if you want to get elected.

So curviness can be an important quality.

This quality was particularly important for this woman who'd been elected in an area known for its strong rural tradition. There they have a better perception of "curvy" women than "skinny" women, who have a metropolitan and bourgeois image.

For this woman, who was always in a good mood, losing weight would irremediably change her relationship with her electors. This was the main brake on her weight loss. It doesn't mean that the next day electors would suddenly stop voting for her. It means that the assets she used to use to achieve success: her charm, her empathy, her curves, her warmness, her humour, wouldn't work as well if she weighted 20kg less.

A SCIENTIFIC EXPERIMENT ABOUT APPEARANCE

A British study conducted by two researchers Swami and Tovée (2012) shows that men's preference for "curves" varied according to their mood and particularly their stress levels.

The aim of the study was to measure the effect of psychological stress on their perception of what makes an attractive woman. Researchers tested 81 heterosexual men. They divided the participants into two groups.

The first group took a test which was known to make people stressed. This test consisted of completing different tasks causing an increase in anxiety, such as undergoing a job interview in front of several people.

The second group was a control group. This group did not take the test causing an increase in stress levels.

The two British researchers then instructed all participants to score 10 images of women's silhouettes, with a range of body mass indicators (BMI), ranging from skinny to obese.

The results of the study are extremely interesting as they show that stressed participants gave significantly higher scores to the fatter women than the unstressed participants.

THE MORE STRESSED MEN ARE, THE MORE ATTRACTED THEY ARE TO CURVY WOMEN.

The two British scientists concluded that physical attraction was sensitive to changes in men's environment. When stressed, men tend to seek security and comfort.

"Curvy" women have a maternal side which makes them more attractive when men are having problems and are stressed. This study confirms the different hypotheses discussed earlier.

HOW CAN YOU CHANGE YOUR IDENTITY?

① RE-LEARNING

Becoming a different person means learning new behaviour, new habits, a new way of thinking: a new philosophy of life! As with any learning process, it needs time. And, as with any learning process, at first you might stumble, commit errors, make mistakes, feel uncomfortable. The position of a learner is never comfortable. That's why some people maintain the same habits and the same ways of thinking throughout their whole life.

By freely choosing to read this book, you've committed to a different path, the path of change. You've agreed to challenge your habits, the way you look at things and your behaviour to evolve towards a different state. Whatever your reasons (health, wellbeing, aesthetics, etc.), you thirst to become a new person, a different person. You've already learnt a lot, but if you want this change to last, you will need to learn much more.

This period has an extremely positive aspect because it allows you to improve. You should never forget the meaning behind what you do. Because you know why you're doing it. Meaning is what you have in your heart, that inexhaustible energy that gives you the strength to climb mountains, reach your limits, overcome any obstacles and take on all challenges. When you know why you're doing something, then you do it. You look straight ahead and move forward.

Learning is an amazing opportunity that life offers you. Remember this! Once you were a child who couldn't walk and was content to crawl along the ground. Now, you walk, you jump and run, without a second thought. Remember this! Once you were a child, unable to talk. And today you use thousands of words to tell hundreds of stories. If you'd refused to learn, you'd still be crawling around going "goo goo".

When you make a lasting and profound change to your lifestyle, you need to learn new behaviours: cooking and eating different foods and different ways of enjoying yourself, doing regular exercise and learning the moves and techniques associated with it, learning to dress, move and comport yourself differently at the same time as managing different behaviour and reactions from your friends and family, learning to manage new emotions, desires and feelings.

Previously in this book I mentioned Rosie, a young woman who'd cheated on her husband after losing 25 kg. She preferred to put all that weight back on again rather than learning:

- Learning how to manage being lusted after men, when no longer protected by her weight,
- Learning to manage their advances, respond to them, turn them away,

- But also learning to manage her own desire and own cravings, her aspirations for adventure and passion in a routine and pretty boring life.

For another person, this might mean learning how to manage new responsibilities in a professional setting. As we saw above, being "skinny" tends to change other people's perception and give off a more credible image. This image encourages superiors to entrust employees with greater responsibilities. For these people, it's also a case of owning the errors and criticisms that a "curvy" person is less subject to, when they used to be more easily forgiven.

It's also necessary to learn how to turn to others, to develop different relationships with them. "Curvy" people are attractive. We trust them. We find them "jolly". We like them almost immediately. All this changes when you lose weight. You need to learn how to create relationships in a different way, using other assets. This won't be easy at first because the person will be judged more strictly, perceived as an adversary or competitor. These are new roles that you must learn to take on.

2 ACCEPTING THAT YOU'VE BECOME SOMEONE ELSE

From the moment people start to see you differently, you've become someone else. And from this arises one of the major obstacles to change:

ATTACHMENT TO YOURSELF.

Most human beings, when it comes to change, will suffer the fear of losing themselves, of no longer knowing where they come from. They're attached to what they are. They're afraid of becoming someone else. When they should let themselves go, relax, let things happen, they rebel and try to stop change. They cling on to what they are because they fear for the future. They're afraid of becoming something they don't recognise, that it's impossible to know: the unknown.

When a caterpillar turns into a butterfly, it becomes a totally different being. And indeed, a caterpillar is nothing like a butterfly. It must be terrifying for a caterpillar to turn into a butterfly. They don't know what it is to fly, they don't know what dangers butterflies face. Crawling about on his its leaf, the caterpillar knows where it lives, its role, what it should eat, who its enemies are. It has its markers. After turning into a butterfly, it loses all of this.

A meeting in Miajima

Recently I went to Japan. I arrived on a small island, near to Hiroshima, which was called Miajima. It was tipping it down. I hadn't booked a hotel. I had no Internet access. I was lost, wandering around the port deciding where to go. And then a woman turned up: a local from the island. She wanted me to follow her. As I'm slightly distrustful by nature, and I like to sort things out myself, I refused. I wanted her to leave me alone.

I just wanted to get online and book a hotel on a site I knew well, find a hotel with a good score that had all the things I expect of a good hotel. I was soaked to my skin, and needed somewhere cosy to rest my head. Above all I wanted to decide where I was going. I wanted to control my future and everything that was to happen in the coming minutes and hours. I had been taught to have power over my life. And then it came to me in a flash. I told myself: just let go. Let life take you where it will!

So I followed this woman. I put my destiny in her hands. She took me to an information point and after chatting with another person in Japanese, she found me a hotel. I'd never have found a hotel online because all the hotels were full that weekend. Then she explained all the wonderful things there were to do on her island, showing me different brochures. She drove me to my hotel in her little car. I don't know why she did it, but she did.

I had a wonderful, stay, walking through verdant forests full of exotic singing birds perched on treetops, visiting Buddhist temples, feeding the thousands of deer that roamed free on that holy island. That day I understood that sometimes you need to stop trying to control everything and let life lead the way.

And you too, if you want the change you undertook by reading this book, and changing your behaviour, to last, must learn to let life take you where it will. Accept that you don't know where your chosen path will lead you. Discover it, be open to opportunities. Because they're certain to arise. By changing your habits, by becoming a different person, you change your destiny. And change always comes with amazing opportunities.

Human beings all too often cling to what they think they are while forgetting a fundamental truth: we don't really decide what we will become. Life does this for us! Our friends and family, the environment we grow up in, events that arise, these are what change us and make us what we are. So you shouldn't be too attached to yourself. Just let events change you, go with the flow, accept things.

STAGE 10:
FEELING AND EMBEDDING CHANGE

STRENGTHEN YOUR BEHAVIOUR AT EACH STAGE

The path to success has numerous stages. You don't lose 10 kg in 1 day. You can't profoundly change your behaviour in 1 week. You advance step by step. And each step taken in the right direction should be a source of immense satisfaction for you. You must learn to reward yourself regularly to encourage your body to stay on the right path. Each time you adopt the right behaviour or the right attitude, reinforce your behaviour.

1 FEEL PROUD OF WHAT YOU'RE ACCOMPLISHING

To reinforce good behaviour, you must learn to reward yourself. I'm talking less of external rewards like buying clothes or doing something you enjoy than internal rewards. Internal rewards are rewards you create yourself, merely by exerting your will. The advantage is that they cost almost nothing, apart from a little time. The first internal reward you can give yourself is:

BE PROUD OF DOING SOMETHING POSITIVE.

Feeling proud is a powerful feeling which releases pleasure hormones throughout our body and mind. Feeling proud mitigates the suffering linked to the efforts made to achieve your objective. Take the time to feel proud when you have accomplished something, when you manage to do regular physical exercise, when you manage not to give in to a craving, when you manage to say "NO THANKS" to a host insisting you eat more than you want.

Self-reinforcement exercise

1/ Close your eyes for a few seconds.
2/ Visualise the act you have achieved.
3/ Let a feeling of pride develop inside you. As you'll see, it's relatively easy.
4/ Just feel proud of what you're doing.
5/ Feel the satisfaction of having accomplished all you have.
6/ Take your time.
7/ Repeat the exercise as many times as possible.
8/ Each time, you should experience a profound feeling of well-being and calm throughout your body.

By doing this exercise, you release pleasure hormones throughout your body. For your brain, these hormones are rewards. When you tame an animal, you give it food or affection when it behaves correctly (for example, when a dolphin jumps out of the water). In this way you reinforce the behaviour you wish to maintain over time. It's a conditioning technique. The miracle is that Man can condition himself. Feeling proud is a reward you give yourself.

In my personal experience, I've noticed that we generally expect rewards from others. We expect recognition from our employer, our spouse or children for what we do for them. And when they don't give this reward, we crave it from them. So the best thing to do is reward yourself. Think about everything you do for them and feel proud of doing all these things.

By learning to reinforce your behaviour in this way, and giving yourself internal rewards, you will become more independent and therefore more free. You'll no longer be beholden on others, preventing frustration and a feeling of missing out. And you will be pleasantly surprised when they reward you by recognising the quality of your work or studies. Nobody can make you as happy and proud as yourself.

2 GIVE YOURSELF PRESENTS

The winner of a competition is awarded a medal, maybe a sum of money and a nice week in the sun. A student who graduates has a right to congratulations from his parents and a nice present in reward. A mountain climber who decides to climb a summit can, once they've conquered it, enjoy a unique view that few can claim to have seen. Whenever we take on a challenge and achieve it, a reward awaits us.

The change you've decided to embark on by reading this book and profoundly changing your behaviour is much more difficult than winning a competition, getting a difficult qualification or climbing a mountain. So once you've achieved your goal, you should give yourself a reward. In addition to being proud of succeeding, treat yourself on the day of your success. The more you enjoy yourself, the more you will associate pleasure with your new behaviour, and the longer it will last.

Treat yourself to the trip of your dreams, buy the clothes you fancy, go and see a show or an artist you love, make love; basically, reward yourself! This will let you embed your new behaviour and make it last. Sub-consciously, your brain and your body will be conditioned to repeat this behaviour in the expectation of pleasure experienced through reward. This is how you can condition yourself to love doing sport or eating vegetables.

MAKE THE MOST
OF THE NEW POSSIBILITIES
OFFERED BY YOUR
NEW BODY

Now your body is lighter. Its physical capacities have developed through physical exercise. You're like a prisoner who's had their ball and chain removed. The time has come to make the most of this new hard won freedom, to make the most of life. Put another way, you will be able to do many things you couldn't do before, and enjoy all the sensations associated with these new practices. It will be an amazing adventure.

When a child starts walking, they discover a new world. Before, they only had access to things on the ground. When they can walk they have access to all the objects placed higher up, and can move further around the house or even outside. This lets them discover new objects, new places, all sorts of stimuli for their imagination and their desire to play. Walking is an amazing tool for exploring the world and learning.

The same thing happens when you lose weight. Before, you could only walk for a short period before getting tired. You couldn't go trekking or cycling because it took too much effort. You rarely see someone who's overweight going diving, sailing or skateboarding. You rarely see an obese person going jogging, doing gymnastics or climbing. Yet these activities are really fun and a source of amazing sensations.

And now you've lost weight, these activities are open to you. You might tell yourself:

THESE ACTIVITIES AREN'T FOR ME.

Get that idea out of your head right away. This is your old idea of yourself. This is your idea of yourself when you were overweight, not the new you who's in shape, full of energy and new abilities. Replace these limiting thoughts and beliefs with positive thoughts, open to the idea of trying new things, exploring, striving. You'll only know if an activity is right for you once you've tried it, once you've experienced its sensations. Then you can have an opinion. Tell yourself:

THESE ACTIVITIES ARE MADE FOR ME.
IN ANY EVENT I'M GOING TO TRY THEM.

If you want your weight loss to be sustainable, you need to try new activities. These new activities are an endless source of pleasure! And this pleasure will quite simply replace the pleasure you got from food. These new activities are in fact your new diet. And they won't make you fat. Quite the contrary, they'll make you move about, and therefore consume calories. They're good for your physical and mental health because they stimulate your body and your imagination.

The time has come to get moving, and above all to explore. The time has come for you, like a child who's just learnt to walk, to explore all the things you have yet to know. Dare to go further, faster, stronger. Dare to discover the things you have yet to know. Stop underestimating your abilities. Whatever your age, your abilities are extraordinary. They're there, sometimes hidden, but there. You just need to call upon them. Nothing is impossible for you.

Otherwise, how can you explain 80-year-old grandfathers running the marathon, or 85-year-old grandmothers doing gymnastics on the bars. These people don't have exceptional physical characteristics. They just believe that they are capable of doing it. As they believe that they are capable of doing it, they do it. As they do it, they train, and their training lets them achieve it. So they tell themselves: I was right, I was capable of it. And they take great pleasure from doing it!

Some activities you can do:

- **Bungee jumping or parachuting:** in tandem, not alone of course, at least when parachuting. There's no risk, and you'll experience some incredible sensations. You'll remember the day you flew for your whole life!

- **Hire or buy a mountain bike and go for a ride in the forest:** what could be nicer than breathing all the oxygen from the forest, feeling the wind on your face as you speed along! What a joy to speed down hills balanced on your bike!

- **Climb a mountain or large hill:** start with a small mountain (500 m) then increase the height and gradient. Challenge yourself to climb every higher! Just wait, the view is magnificent from the top!

- **Go canoeing or kayaking:** a river, a lovely summer's day, and you can paddle off for the whole day! And why not stop on the way for a picnic. Make it extra special by doing it with your family!

- **Circumnavigate an island or cross it on foot:** a long walk with a goal, that of crossing or circumnavigating an island! Lovely beaches, beautiful cliffs, at the end of the day you'll be left with some wonderful images!

- **Go jogging:** some good shoes, a forest, and a 45 minute run. You stop when you want! You feel your heart beating, your lungs filling with oxygen, followed by a nice hot shower for guaranteed pleasure!

DISCOVER NEW FOODS AND NEW PRACTICES

You can continuously change your diet by discovering new products. Personally, when I was trying to lose weight I remember discovering Quinoa and Buckwheat, two delicious plants, then rapeseed oil, rich in omega-3. I also learnt to cook and eat aubergines and carrots in different shapes and forms. Food is ripe for discovery. Be curious, deepen your knowledge and always improve your diet if you want to make progress.

This involves the discovery of new fruits and vegetables by tasting and exploring. The body is a great tool for exploring the world, as is the tongue. By discovering new flavours, by learning new tastes for healthy foods, you will move one step further on the path to health. There are thousands of foods yet to be discovered, not to mention spices, aromatics, herbs and different cooking methods. Testing and exploring is the perfect way of experiencing different pleasures!

In addition to food, why not try new eating practices. Here are three practices you can try if you feel like it!

❶ DO A FAST

I must admit I've never tried it, but I've considered it because a lot of people I know have done it. What's interesting in terms of diet and life in general is trying. So I recommend you try fasting. The benefits of fasting have been known since antiquity. It allows the body, and above all the digestive system, to rest (40% of the energy consumed by the body is spent on digestion!) This break causes changes to your cellular metabolism which can have health benefits.

The benefits of a therapeutic fast were particularly well studied in the Soviet Union between the 60s and the 90s. Studies showed that fasting can have a positive effect on skin conditions, hypertension, chronic inflammatory ailments, allergies, chest conditions (asthma) or digestive conditions. Also, fasting has a beneficial effect on psychological health because when fasting the body produces hormones that calm and relax the body.

❷ GO VEGETARIAN

You could also try going vegetarian. Meat is not an essential food because there are very many other sources of vegetable proteins (soya, lentils, quinoa). I personally recently became a vegetarian, or rather a flexitarian. I only eat meal on special occasions such as family meals. Eating vegetarian food has given me greater inner calm and better digestion. It's also excellent for the planet because livestock farms are a huge source of pollution.

Trying doesn't necessarily mean adopting. You should never feel obliged to rigorously confirm to a diet. A good diet needs certain markers but also flexibility and freedom. If your body feels the need to eat meat, cheese or eggs, it means you need the nutrients contained in these foods. In this case, you should eat them. Just pay attention to the origin of these foods to ensure you eat quality food.

③ EAT RAW VEGETABLES

Some people only eat raw foods, particularly fruits and vegetables. Without embarking on a strict new diet, whose long term consequences you're unaware of, why not try a cure. Make the most of summer and spend a week eating only raw vegetables and eating only fresh fruit and vegetables: tomatoes, peppers, cucumbers, courgettes, cherries, peaches, watermelon etc. This food, rich in vitamin C and water, is the ideal way to feel good when it's hot.

Such a diet, accompanied by a physical activity, will let you unwind over the holidays and get rid of the stress of the last year. Why not try different diets such as the Cretan diet, based on fruits, vegetables, fish, soft cheese and olive oil, with few sugary foods. This diet is also perfect for a week in the sun. A delight for the body and your taste buds. A great way of combining pleasure and health!

THE LAST WORD

Now we've reached the end of this book. This ending is the beginning of a new life. This new life is different from the one you would have lived if you hadn't read this book, there is every chance of it being longer and more fulfilled. Now you're one of those new epicureans, those people who make the most of life at the same time as really loving and respecting their body. You are open to all the pleasures of life but above all seek wellbeing and health.

By following the teachings in this book, you've made the necessary changes to your life. You've made a lasting change to your habits, your behaviour, the way you think, your reflexes. You've changed your identity, your values and what defines you to yourself and others. You've had to (and will still have to) manage the tensions caused by your changing relationships with your friends, colleagues and family. By doing all this, you need to recognise you've achieved something amazing.

Today's society is all about great exploits: climbing Everest, rowing across the Atlantic or swimming the Channel, making a great scientific, technical or medical discovery etc. But there are some things which are much more difficult than those I've mentioned, and which often go unnoticed: one of them is called changing. Because nobody's prepared, trained, taught to change. Changing is one of the most difficult human challenges ever.

- The first thing you should do when looking back on the thing you've achieved is to feel proud. Whatever the total amount of weight lost, you should feel proud of the path you've travelled.

- The second thing is to accept my congratulations. Having walked this path myself, I know how difficult it is. Also, I must congratulate you personally for this success.

- The third thing is to accept the thanks of all the people who participate and will participate in this program. You will serve as an example for them. An example inspires and convinces more than a thousand words.

By changing your behaviour for good, you're doing much more than creating the conditions for your own happiness. You're opening the way to many others who, in the future, will want to follow you. Not only will you live longer and healthier, but you will allow other people to take the same path. By following this program and ensuring the changes you've made are lasting, you'll help hundreds of people to improve their health and life a longer, happier life.

When you start to doubt, when you go through a difficult period or feel the need to eat more, or eat badly, remember your commitment. By choosing to read this book you've made a lasting commitment to yourself to eat healthily and develop healthy habits. Now you've done it, you've made a commitment not only to yourself, but also to all the other people that are suffering, and for whom you now represent hope.

That's why you can't cave in! That's why you need to continue this behaviour for good, because now you know where your responsibility lies. Your actions are of great importance for the health and wellbeing of hundreds of other people. By changing your behaviour for good, you're avoiding a ton of illnesses and suffering. You'll be like a doctor without any medical know-how, caring and soothing merely by example.

The way we work forces us to be sedentary, while adverts of all stripes underhandedly work for supermarkets and the agro-food industry to influence and manipulate you and convince you that bad foods are good foods. Not to mention French culture, which has replaced God and Catholicism with food and drink. Everything mitigates against what you've just achieved, yet you did it. Bravo! You're great! You've achieved something amazing!

Close your eyes, take a deep breath, feel proud of what you've accomplished, reward yourself. Accept my sincerest congratulations and savour this moment (it will replace hundreds of fatty, sugary cakes). Feel your responsibility from now on to care for your body and stand as an example, an example that cares, fights, prevents and helps. What you've accomplished is a huge achievement for you and for everyone.

I want you to be happy for the rest of your life. I want you to be as light as a feather, and fly towards your dreams. And I also want you to spread this lightness, this joy and this happiness all around, and to share it with the greatest number of people. One last time, be proud, be happy, be self-assured. Until we meet again: in another book, at a conference or on social media. I'll end with this phase from Gandhi: "Be the change you wish to see in the world."

BIBLIOGRAPHY

Amadieu, J.-F. (2005). *Le poids des apparences : beauté, amour et gloire.* Paris : Odile Jacob.

Akbaraly, T., Brunner, E., & al. (2009). *Dietary pattern and depressive symptoms in middle age*, The British Journal of Psychiatry. Oct. 195 (5). pp. 408-413.

Benton, D. (2007). *The impact of diet on anti-social, violent and criminal behavior. Neurosciences and Biobehavioral Reviews.* Vol. 31(5). pp. 752-774.

McCann, D., & al. (2007). *Food Additives and Hyperactive Behaviour in 3-Year-Old and 8/9-Year-Old Children in the Community : A Randomised, Double-Blinded, Placebo-Controlled Trial.* Lancet (Nov. 3) : Vol. 370. No. 9598. pp. 1560–67.

Greeno, C. G., &Wing, R. R. (1994). *Stress-induced eating. Psychological Bulletin.* 115. pp. 444-464.

Gesch, B., & al. (2002). *Influence of supplementary vitamins, mineral and essential fatty acids on the antisocial behaviour of young adult prisoners.* The British Journal of Psychiatry. 181 (1). pp 22-28.

Laitinen, J., & Sovio, U. (2002) *Stress-related eating and drinking behaviour and body mass index and predictors of this behaviour.* Preventive Medicine. 34. pp. 29-39.

Lattimore, P., & Caswell, N. (2004). *Differential effects of active and passive stress on food intake in restrained and unrestrained eaters Appetite.* 42. pp. 167-173.

Lenoir, M., & al. (2007). *Intense sweetness surpasses cocaine reward.* PLoSOne. 8 : e698.

Moore, S., & al. (2009). *Confectionary consumption in childhood and adult violence. British Journal of Psychiatry.* Vol. 195. pp. 366-367.

Polivy, J., & Hermam, C. P. (1999). *Distress and dieting: why do dieters overeat? International Journal of Eating Disorder.* 25. pp. 153-164.

Schab, D. W., & al. (2004). *Do Artificial Food Colors Promote Hyperactivity in Children with Hyperactive Syndromes? A Meta-Analysis of Double-Blind Placebo-Controlled Trials.* Journal of Developmental and Behavioral Pediatrics. Vol. 25 (Dec.). No. 6. pp. 423–34.

Swami, V., & Tovée, M-J. (2012). *The Impact of Psychological Stress on Men's Judgements of Female Body Size.* PLoS One. 7(8).

Zaalberg, A., & al. (2010). *Effects of nutritional supplements on aggression, rule-breaking, and psychopathology among young adult prisoners.* Aggressive behavior. Vol. 36. pp. 117-126.